What Do You Know About Sex?

Diane Zahler
Kathy A. Zahler

Reviewed by
Juanita Jenyons, M.D.
Board Certified in OB-GYN
Diplomate of the American Board of
Obstetrics and Gynecology

New York   London   Toronto   Sydney   Tokyo   Singapore

This book is a reference work based on research by the authors. The medical information contained herein is not intended to replace the services of a trained health professional; if a medical or sexual problem is suspected, the authors and the publisher urge the reader to seek the advice of a such a professional.

PRENTICE HALL

15 Columbus Circle
New York, NY 10023

An Arco Book

Manufactured in the United States of America

Contents

Acknowledgments / iv

Introduction / 1

Scoring Key / 8

TEST 1   Ex Ovo Omnia: The Female Body / 9

TEST 2   What a Piece of Work: The Male Body / 35

TEST 3   The Big O: Human Sexuality / 57

TEST 4   In the Family Way: Pregnancy and Childbirth / 81

TEST 5   Stop! In the Name of Love: Contraception / 107

TEST 6   Let's Get Tested: Sexually Transmitted Diseases / 133

TEST 7   Sacred and Profane: Licit and Illicit Sex / 159

TEST 8   Back to the Garden: Sex in Cultural History / 185

Bibliography / 215

Acknowledgments

This one is for Jan and Stan, without whom
(we now know) we would not be here.

Thanks also to PS, CC, CH, RZ, MK, SH, and PZ.

Introduction

The first thing you learn when you write a book called *What Do You Know About Sex?* is that everyone thinks the answer is "everything." Here's a subject on which everyone has an opinion, from the sales manager who thinks that our bookjacket is too risqué for his clients to the scientist who encourages us to consider the divine mystery that attends the sexual process, from people who think the tone should be high-minded and clinical to others who insist that any quiz book on sex must be salaciously humorous, with the mood and style of a toga party.

What's the big deal about sex, anyway? For me, the matter of interest in writing about sex is determining that line that separates public from private. Perhaps the justices of the Supreme Court would agree. Diane sits in front of her word processor, banging out text on herpes and muttering, "The history of sex *is* the history of disease." Perhaps the people who run the AIDS hotline at the Centers for Disease Control would agree. For a geneticist we know, sex is the process that ensures that we won't precisely replicate either one of our parents. This fact intrigues and delights him, and we find that endearing and even unselfish; he is our father, and the process in our case has meant that we can be female and have our mother's eyes.

It's amazing how complicated things get once you take away the estrous cycle and make sex pleasurable as well as organic. Suddenly, sex is possible even when conception is not. You can do it at any time of the month. You can do it when you're old. You can do it with someone of your own sex, or you can do it all by yourself. You can even bide your time and do it with someone you love. It's a lot more interesting to be human than to be, say, a goldfish. Or a flatworm. Or an amoeba. On the other hand, we've got problems none of them can touch.

Take morality. If you *can* have sex without procreating, does that mean you should? This question has plagued us since we first discovered that one act led to the other. If you *can* have sex with anyone at any time, should you just go for it? Take violence. In some species, rape is physically impossible; we have the unfortunate ability to engage in forcible sex. Take disease. The nature of our sex act, the position and structure of our genitals, the frequency with which we engage in sex, and our tendency to have more than one partner mean that we are prone to transmitting bacteria, protozoa, and viruses sexually.

When it comes to sex, we have more choices than do goldfish, flatworms, or amoebae. Informed choices depend on information. To be a responsible sexual being in this day and age, you must know a lot about sex. You must know how it happens and what it means. You must know causes and effects. You must know what is legal and what is not. You must know how pregnancies occur and how they are prevented. You must know how to protect yourself and your partner from diseases that can kill you both.

Things are easier for the lower species. But would you care to trade bliss for simplicity? After all, as Mae West once said, "Too much of a good thing. . .can be wonderful."

The Tests

Test 1: The Female Body

In the body of a human female, a good deal of time and energy is spent in producing ripe eggs. For over 30 years, eggs mature and are released at the rate of about one a month. Timing is everything, at least in terms of the continuation of the species — there is a window of opportunity each month during which the ripe egg may be fertilized. This test looks at your knowledge of the structure of the female sex organs and the (mostly hormonal) signals that control them; we also examine some of the things that can go wrong with this finely tuned mechanism.

Test 2: The Male Body

The male contribution to human sexual reproduction, to paraphrase Carl Sagan, is "billions and billions of sperm." The competitive nature that we are all too often told is peculiarly male shows up at the microscopic level in ejaculation. A single ejaculation contains hundreds of millions of sperm, all competing to reach the egg and be the lucky one to fertilize it. In this test we review some of the complicated structures and hormonal controls that govern the reproductive process in men.

Test 3: Human Sexuality

So what if Nature invented sexual intercourse as a means of propagating the species — the main thing about sex, as far as human beings are concerned, is that it's fun. We are a species without an estrous cycle; human females are always (at least potentially) receptive. That puts us one up on most animals. So does the fact that human males don't just ejaculate, they have orgasms, and human females can have orgasms, too. Take away the biological imperative, and what's left? Pleasure. Well, pleasure and its related complications — embarrassment, guilt, morality, etiquette, the wet spot. . . . This test touches on the complications but deals primarily with the forms and physiology of sexual pleasure.

Test 4: Pregnancy and Childbirth

A ripe egg is moving blithely down the Fallopian tube when it is boldly accosted by the fastest sperm in a pack of millions. The fertilized egg, now called an embryo, proceeds to the uterus and begins immediately to develop into the many-celled, complex organism that will finally emerge nine months later as a human baby. This test examines the astonishing changes that take place in the embryo/fetus and in its host, the mother, along the path to childbirth.

Test 5: Contraception

One of the complications that comes with enjoyment of sex is the fact that you might just want to enjoy it *without* making a baby. That's simple enough if you stick to partners of the same sex, but if you are heterosexual, you may need to take special precautions. We tend to associate contraception with the so-called sexual revolution of the 1960s, but in fact, we've had methods of interfering with conception and terminating pregnancy for thousands of years. Frankly, we don't have all that many more types of contraceptives now than we did in Biblical times, but those we do have are a bit more effective. Test 5 examines your knowledge of modern contraceptives, their uses, effectiveness, and potential side effects.

Test 6: Sexually Transmitted Diseases

Maybe the history of sex isn't *precisely* the history of disease, but there is an awful array of diseases that can be spread through sexual contact. Humans enjoy sex, so they want to engage in it frequently, and that ups their chances of spreading disease. Many humans are monogamous, but many have more than one partner, and that ups their risk of disease even more. If there is one test in this book you should want to ace, this is the one. We test your understanding of the major sexually transmitted diseases, their symptoms, methods of transmission, and potential cures, if any.

Test 7: Licit and Illicit Sex

Human beings are strange: no sooner do we gain the freedom to engage in mutually satisfying sex anytime we like than we try like mad to restrict that freedom. Throughout recorded history, sexual activity and social mores have danced a nervous tango — first one leads, then the other. The societies most repressive in public tend to harbor the most licentious activities in private. In this test, we explore today's public laws and regulations regarding the most private of activities and take a look at some new ethical questions that may lead to legislation in the years to come.

Test 8: Sex in Cultural History

There's nothing new under the sun. Your favorite sexual position, the one you think is so outrageous, probably turns up in the pornographic art of fifth century B.C. Athens. The scandalous sex club your best friend visited in Vegas doesn't even compare to the wild romps regularly engaged in by the seventeenth century Adamites. On the other hand, how *did* people in ancient times explain conception? Where do we get our notions about what is and is not proper behavior? Test 8 looks back and tests your knowledge of sex in history and in other cultures.

How to Take the Tests

Each of the eight tests has forty questions. The items are multiple-choice, and four possibilities are listed for each:

34. If a woman forgets to take the Pill on Friday, she should
  a. take a pill on Saturday and omit one pill at the end of the cycle
  b. start knitting booties
  c. take two pills on Saturday
  d. stop taking pills until the next cycle begins

You may know the answer right off the bat, or you may be able to come up with the right answer through a process of elimination.

When you complete a test, use the explanatory answers that follow the test to check your responses. The answers will help you determine *why* your response was correct or incorrect and may increase your knowledge of the subject.

34. (c) It's not recommended, but it is possible to play "catch-up" with the Pill as long as only one or two pills have been missed. If two pills have been missed, a woman can take two one day and two the next to catch up, but should probably also use spermicide or a barrier method of contraception for the rest of the cycle just to make sure.

Use the Scoring Key that follows this introduction to grade yourself. What you will probably find is that you do very well on certain tests and less well on others. The tests you should be most concerned about are probably Tests 4, 5, and 6; these are the areas in which ignorance could mean the difference between conception and contraception, and between life and death.

Our suggestion: Take the tests with your partner. Read the explanatory answers aloud. Talk about your areas of sexual illiteracy. Marvel at facts that are new to you. Try the recommended works in our bibliography. Learn together. Ignorance was required in the Garden of Eden, but in today's world, knowledge is *not* our downfall, but is instead our strength.

KAZahler

January 24, 1991

Scoring Key

Score one point for each correct answer.

35–40   *Excellent.* Do you spend your spare time reading back issues of the *New England Journal of Medicine* and taking notes on the *Kama-sutra*? Your knowledge may unnerve your friends.

30–34   *Good.* Not only did you pay attention in your eighth grade health class, but you've been a quick study ever since.

25–29   *Fair.* Are you still living the sex life you lived in the seventies? It may be time for a reality check-up.

20–24   *Poor.* Let's hope your partner knows more than you do. If not, you may both be in trouble.

Below 20   *Irresponsible.* Your ignorance may be hazardous to your health and/or life-style. See the bibliography in the back of this book.

Ex Ovo Omnia: The Female Body

*One is not born a woman,
one becomes one.*

— *SIMONE DE BEAUVOIR*

TEST 1

Ex Ovo Omnia:
The Female Body

One is not born a woman,
one becomes one.

— SIMONE DE BEAUVOIR

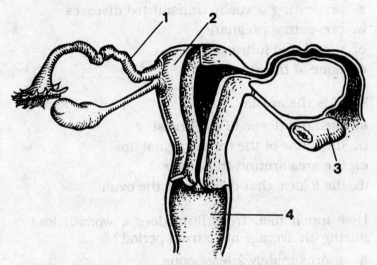

1. What is the part of the body labeled 1?

    a. vagina

    b. Fallopian tube

    c. ovary

    d. uterus

2. What is the part of the body labeled 2?

    a. ovary

    b. vagina

    c. Fallopian tube

    d. uterus

3. What is the part of the body labeled 3?

    a. vagina

    b. uterus

    c. ovary

    d. Fallopian tube

4. Douching can be useful in

   a. preventing sexually transmitted diseases

   b. preventing pregnancy

   c. increasing lubrication

   d. none of the above

5. What is the areola?

   a. the fatty tissue of the breast

   b. the name of the inner vaginal lips

   c. the area around the nipple

   d. the follicle that discharges the ovum

6. How much menstrual fluid does a woman lose during an average menstrual period?

   a. approximately 2 teaspoons

   b. approximately 3 tablespoons

   c. approximately 6 tablespoons

   d. approximately 1 cup

7. What glands control ovulation?

   a. the pineal, the thyroid, and the ovary

   b. the pituitary and the adrenal

   c. the parathyroid and the thyroid

   d. the hypothalamus, the pituitary, and the ovary

8. What are some appropriate reasons for hysterectomy?

   a. prolapsed uterus, ovarian cancer, or bleeding fibroids

   b. abortion, sterilization, or menstrual irregularity

    c. bladder infections, cervicitis, or ectopic pregnancy

    d. vaginitis, trichomoniasis, or genital herpes

9. What percentage of American women will contract breast cancer?

    a. about 40%

    b. about 10%

    c. about 5%

    d. about 1%

10. Why is endometriosis often called "the career woman's disease"?

    a. It has been linked to the use of video display terminals.

    b. It often appears in women in their 20s and 30s who have delayed childbirth.

    c. It is the result of on-the-job stress.

    d. It only appears in women who have worked outside the home.

11. What are some causes of amenorrhea?

    a. frequent intercourse or severe cramps

    b. insomnia or depression

    c. too much caffeine or use of barrier contraception

    d. excessive weight loss or breastfeeding

12. For what was the drug DES used?

    a. to prevent morning sickness

    b. as a "morning after" pill

    c. to prevent miscarriage

    d. to prevent breast cancer

13. On which of these body parts do women often develop cysts?

   a. vagina and Fallopian tubes

   b. ovary and breast

   c. nipple and labia

   d. cervix and clitoris

14. Which of these changes is linked with puberty?

   a. Irrational anger at parents develops.

   b. The vagina becomes longer.

   c. The body manufactures estrogen.

   d. all of the above

15. What is the main cause of menstrual cramps?

   a. a high level of prostaglandins

   b. too much blood in the uterus

   c. a sedentary lifestyle

   d. low levels of dietary calcium

16. What role do male hormones (androgens) play in female puberty?

   a. They contribute to breast growth.

   b. They cause fatty deposits on the hips and thighs.

   c. They cause acne and the growth of body hair.

   d. all of the above

17. How often should a woman examine her breasts to check for lumps or any changes?

   a. once a year, from puberty on

   b. once a year, after age 35

   c. every month, from puberty on

   d. twice a day, after menopause

18. How does the ovum move through the Fallopian tube?

    a. Gravity moves the ovum downward.

    b. Cramps cause the Fallopian tube to squeeze the ovum down.

    c. Hairs called cilia move the ovum downward.

    d. The force of the ovum's release from the ovary moves it downward.

19. What changes occur in the vagina after menopause?

    a. The vagina lengthens and becomes tighter.

    b. The vagina becomes moister and more prone to infection.

    c. The vagina becomes drier and less elastic.

    d. The vagina does not change after menopause.

20. Which of these statements about tampons is correct?

    a. A virgin should not use tampons.

    b. A woman can use tampons during any normal menstrual period.

    c. A woman trying to conceive should not use tampons during her period.

    d. A woman should not use tampons during the first year she menstruates.

21. Can a young girl become pregnant before her first menstruation?

    a. Yes, if she has previously ovulated.

    b. No, menstruation is the first sign of fertility.

    c. No, girls are rarely fertile before age thirteen.

    d. Yes, if her growth spurt is complete.

22. Where is the clitoris located?

    a. deep within the vagina, near the cervix

    b. at the opening of the vagina

    c. between the urethral opening and the pubic mound

    d. No one really knows.

23. Which of the following is *not* true of the vagina?

    a. It contains sensitive nerve endings along its length.

    b. Its walls secrete fluids.

    c. In a woman who is not aroused, its walls touch each other.

    d. It is three or four inches long.

24. What do technicians look for in a Pap smear test?

    a. abnormal cells

    b. syphilis-causing bacteria

    c. chancres or genital warts

    d. all of the above

25. Fibroid tumors are most likely to be found

    a. along the vaginal walls

    b. in the wall of the uterus

    c. encircling one or both ovaries

    d. in the Fallopian tubes

26. Which hormone prepares a woman's body for pregnancy?

    a. testosterone

    b. estrogen

    c. androgen

    d. progesterone

27. Which of these diagrams best illustrates a typical menstrual cycle?

a.

Ovulation 1	2	3	4	5	6	7
8	9	**M e** 10	**n s t r** 11	**u a l** 12	**p e r** 13	**i o d** 14
Menstrual period 15	Ovulation 1					

b.

M e 1	**n s t r** 2	**u a l** 3	**p e r** 4	**i o d** 5	6	7
8	9	10	11	12	13	Ovulation 14
15	16	17	18	19	20	21
22	23	24	25	26	27	28
M e 1	**n s t r** 2	**u a l** 3	**p e r** 4	**i o d** 5	6	7

c.

1	2	3	4	5	6	7
8	9	Ovulation 10	11	12	13	14
M e n s t r u a l p e r i o d 15	16	17	18	19	20	21
22	23	24	25	26	27	28
29	30	31	Ovulation 1	2	3	4

d.

28. When does a woman's body begin manufacturing eggs?
- **a.** before her birth
- **b.** at about age 9 or 10
- **c.** a few months before her first menstruation
- **d.** after her first menstruation

29. In order for a human baby to be born female,
- **a.** her father's fertilizing sperm must contain an X chromosome
- **b.** her mother's egg cell must contain an XX chromosome pair
- **c.** all male organs must remain undeveloped in the fetus
- **d.** her mother's egg cell must contain 46 chromosomes

30. What determines the size and shape of a woman's breasts?
- **a.** height
- **b.** age at puberty
- **c.** heredity
- **d.** all of the above

31. Reduced sexual desire following a hysterectomy may be due to
- **a.** depression
- **b.** decreased hormone levels
- **c.** nerve damage
- **d.** all of the above

32. Congestion of blood vessels, fluid retention, and a drop in hormone levels can lead to the condition known as

    a. uterine prolapse

    b. trichomoniasis

    c. premenstrual syndrome

    d. climacteric

33. The cervix is the passageway between

    a. the vagina and the labia

    b. the ovary and the uterus

    c. the urethra and the bladder

    d. the uterus and the vagina

34. Synthetic estrogen is occasionally prescribed

    a. as a component in birth control pills

    b. to reduce depression in menopausal patients

    c. to prevent osteoporosis

    d. all of the above

35. When a woman is sexually aroused, her Bartholin's glands

    a. release estrogen into her bloodstream

    b. produce mucus in the cervix

    c. secrete fluid along the labia

    d. retract the hood of the clitoris

36. In a woman who is a virgin, the hymen

    a. completely seals the vaginal canal

    b. may be stretched, but always remains unbroken

    c. may or may not be broken

    d. retracts during menstruation but otherwise remains intact

37. Which of the following would *not* be a standard part of a pelvic exam?

   a. a Pap smear

   b. an examination of the vulva

   c. palpation of the uterus

   d. dilation and curettage (D and C)

38. For whom is the risk of toxic-shock syndrome highest?

   a. menstruating women older than 35

   b. menstruating women younger than 30

   c. women who are using tampons for the first time

   d. women who have had at least one child

39. During menstruation, a woman should *not*

   a. ride a horse

   b. have unprotected intercourse if she does not want a child

   c. work out with weights or play organized sports

   d. take a hot bath or swim in a pool

40. After menopause,

   a. the ovaries no longer produce ripe eggs

   b. the uterine lining fails to thicken and slough off

   c. estrogen production declines but does not cease

   d. all of the above

TEST 1: Explanatory Answers

1. **(b)** Also known as oviducts (egg tubes), the Fallopian tubes connect the ovaries and the uterus. Each is about four inches long and as narrow as a pin. They do not directly adjoin the ovaries but bend around them, and finger-like extensions called fimbriae help move the egg from the ovary to the tube.

2. **(d)** The uterus, or womb, is a fist-sized organ that is made of muscle. Its interior is lined with endometrial tissue, which is discharged during menses. When a woman is not pregnant, the walls of the uterus touch, but because of its muscular structure, it is capable of great expansion during pregnancy.

3. **(c)** The ovaries are walnut-sized glands that contain a woman's lifetime supply of eggs, or ova. After puberty, one (or, rarely, two or more) of these eggs is released during each menstrual cycle. The ovaries also produce hormones that regulate sexual development.

4. **(d)** Under ordinary circumstances, douching, or washing the vagina with a liquid solution, is not necessary. The vagina "washes" itself with fluids, and some douche ingredients can actually cause infection. The common belief that douching with carbonated beverages can prevent pregnancy is erroneous, and some specialists posit that the practice can cause a fatal embolism.

5. **(c)** The darker skin at the tip of the breast is made up of the areola and the nipple. The areola contains oil glands that may cause small surface bumps; during pregnancy these glands produce oil that protects the nipple when a woman nurses. Because the only muscles in the breast are under the nipple and areola, these areas can become erect when exposed to cold, when touched, or when a woman becomes sexually aroused. However, a woman can have inverted nipples, a normal condition if evident since puberty, which is caused by short milk ducts that pull the nipples inward.

6. **(c)** Menstrual fluid consists of blood, mucus, endometrial fragments, and vaginal secretions. In an average period, the amount lost is about 6 tablespoons, or 3 ounces. However, the total amount can range from 1 tablespoon to nearly a full cup, and a particular woman's flow can vary greatly in amount from month to month.

7. **(d)** Ovulation, or the release of an egg or eggs by the ovary, is controlled by hormones in a woman's body. As estrogen levels drop each month, the hypothalamus gland produces gonadotrophin-releasing hormone, or GnRH. This signals the pituitary gland to produce FSH, follicle-stimulating hormone, which causes one ovary to form 10 to 20 egg sacs or follicles. Of these, only one or two will develop completely. The follicle makes estrogen, signaling the formation of more GnRH, FSH, and LH, or luteinizing hormone. When these hormones peak, the ovary releases the egg. This stage of the menstrual cycle lasts about a week.

8. **(a)** A hysterectomy is major surgery involving removal of a woman's reproductive organs. Although it is estimated that more than 40% of women will have hysterectomies by age 65, critics claim that up to half of these operations are unnecessary. Only 20% of hysterectomies in the United States are performed in response to life-threatening conditions. In the South, according to the authors of *Our Bodies, Ourselves*, there have been many cases of black women and poor white women given hysterectomies for the purpose of sterilization without their knowledge, the so-called "Mississippi Appendectomy." A hysterectomy can involve the removal of only the uterus, or of the uterus and cervix.

9. **(b)** Current estimates hold that one in nine women in the United States will develop breast cancer. Only 1% of breast cancer cases are men. If discovered early, 85% of women survive five years after diagnosis. Treatments range from lumpectomy — removal of the tumor and surrounding tissue — to radical mastectomy — re-

moval of the breast, surrounding chest muscles, and nearby lymph nodes. A study published in 1985 revealed that in women whose cancer had not spread to their lymph nodes, ten-year survival rates were the same whether they had radical mastectomies, simple mastectomies (removal of the breast but not the muscles or lymph nodes) with radiation therapy, or simple mastectomies without radiation, leading researchers to conclude that extensive surgery was not usually advantageous.

10. **(b)** Endometriosis is a disease in which the uterine lining grows and sometimes bleeds outside the uterus, causing scarring, lesions, cysts, and nodules. It can result in severe pain during menstruation, ovulation, and intercourse. Some possible causes of endometriosis include trauma from surgery; development of tissue existing before a woman's own birth; and reflux of menstrual fluid. The disease can start just after puberty but is most prevalent (or most often reported and diagnosed) in women in their 20s and 30s, leading to the erroneous label "the career woman's disease." Pregnancy can temporarily halt or relieve endometriosis, but in most cases it is a progressive, chronic condition that can only be controlled by hormonal treatments or surgery.

11. **(d)** Amenorrhea, or absence of menstruation, is divided into two categories. Primary amenorrhea occurs when a woman has never had a period. Secondary amenorrhea occurs when menstruation stops after at least one period. Loss of weight, linked with dieting or excessive exercise, can cause this condition by lowering the body-fat ratio and causing hormonal changes. However, recent studies of female runners reported in the *New England Journal of Medicine* suggest that exercise alone does not lead to menstrual irregularity. Pregnancy, breastfeeding, use of birth control pills, and stress are other causes.

12. **(c)** DES, or diethylstilbestrol, was commonly prescribed in the 1940s, '50s, and '60s to prevent miscarriage. By the 1950s, studies showed that the drug was ineffective, but until the FDA advised against it in 1971, it was still used. Daughters exposed to DES in the womb have a higher than average incidence of vaginal and some cervical cancers as well as structural abnormalities of the cervix, vagina, and uterus. Sons exposed to the drug have higher rates of undescended testicles and low sperm counts. Women who took DES have a higher than average incidence of breast cancer.

13. **(b)** Cysts are small sacs filled with fluid or other materials. The most common sites for cysts are the breasts (fibrocystic breast disease) and the ovaries. These cysts are of particular concern to women because they can mimic or even develop into cancer. Cysts can cause discomfort or pain, and some ovarian cysts release hormones that have masculinizing effects including hirsutism (excessive growth of facial and body hair), obesity, and difficulty getting pregnant; or feminizing effects including early puberty, heavy menstrual bleeding, and irregular periods.

14. **(d)** As a girl approaches puberty, her body prepares itself for having sex and giving birth. Her vagina lengthens, her cervix grows, hormonal levels rise and ovulation occurs, and menstruation starts. The changes of puberty are triggered by the hypothalamus gland, but it is unclear what signals the hypothalamus to begin the process.

15. **(a)** Although some women experience cramps caused by specific medical problems, most menstrual cramps (primary dysmenorrhea) are caused by hormones called prostaglandins, which cause the uterus to contract. Most women with painful cramps have high levels of prostaglandins; some researchers believe that if these hormones enter the intestinal tract, they can also cause nausea, diarrhea, and vomiting. Anti-prostaglandin medications are often helpful in relieving cramps and other associated symptoms.

16. **(c)** The adrenal glands produce androgens in both men and women. As estrogen levels in women rise, androgens stimulate growth and cause pubic and underarm hair to grow. Androgen levels fall after puberty, and in those women who have had androgen-related acne, the condition often clears up.

17. **(c)** Though the majority of women do not examine their breasts, doctors recommend a monthly self-examination from puberty onward. The best time for this examination is just after menstruation, since before the period breasts can be swollen or lumpy. In addition, women are advised to get a baseline mammogram (breast X-ray) between the ages of 35 and 40, and to have one every two years from 40 to 50 and every year thereafter.

18. **(c)** As the ovum enters the Fallopian tube with help from the fimbria, tiny hairlike cilia take over. These cilia are attached to muscles in the tube, and as the muscles contract, the cilia wave, moving the egg slowly toward the uterus, a journey taking approximately one week.

19. **(c)** Menopause, which ordinarily begins between ages 45 and 55, is the cessation of menstruation. Vaginal atrophy, or dryness and thinning of the vaginal walls, is an effect of lower estrogen levels after menopause. Atrophy can make arousal time longer and intercourse less comfortable, but many women find this problem is offset by the freedom from worry about pregnancy and feel that sexual intercourse is even more satisfying than in their pre-menopausal years.

20. **(b)** When a girl first begins to menstruate, her vagina may be tight and her hymen may have only a small opening. However, even these young women can stretch their vaginal openings so that tampon use is comfortable. Contrary to popular belief, virgins can use tampons. Not all virgins have hymens, and among those who do, many stretch or break them in day-to-day activity. Even an untorn hymen has openings that allow menstrual blood and other fluids to flow out, making tampon use possible.

21. **(a)** Although it is rare for a young girl to ovulate, or discharge an egg, before her very first menstruation, it does occasionally happen, and thus a girl who is sexually active may become pregnant before she has even officially reached puberty. The standard range for the onset of menses, called *menarche*, is from age 10 to age 16. Sometimes ovulation does not take place for months after the first menstruation, even when all other signs point to regular periods, but the fact that it can occur before menarche means that *all* sexually active girls of any age should take precautions or risk pregnancy.

22. **(c)** The clitoris is a small organ located in front of the opening that leads from the bladder. With sexual stimulation, it becomes erect, and its sensitive nerve endings make it the primary source of pleasure in female sexual response.

23. **(a)** The vagina is not a particularly sensitive part of the body. Most women experience sensitivity only along the outer third of the vaginal canal. If it *were* very sensitive, childbirth might be even more painful, for besides being the sexual passageway, the vagina is also the birth canal down which a baby travels from the uterus. In its standard unaroused position, the vagina is a collapsed tube about three or four inches long, extending at a 45-degree angle from the vaginal opening toward the small of the back. Its most vital qualities in terms of sexual intercourse are its abilities to stretch and to lubricate itself.

24. **(a)** The Pap test, named for the gynecologist George Papanicolaou, is used to test for the presence of abnormal cells on the cervix. A swab, brush, or spatula is used to take a sample of mucus by scraping along the

surface of the opening of the uterus. The sample is observed under a microscope and rated by a technician. Different rating systems are used, but often a Roman numeral I indicates that no abnormal cells are seen. The numeral II means that some cells look unusual or inflamed. A Class III rating indicates atypical cells, or dysplasia, potentially a precancerous condition, and Classes IV and V indicate the existence of cancer cells. In an average year, according to *Smart Medicine*, 90% of test results are Class I, 5 to 6% are Class II, 3 to 4% are Class III, and only about 0.1% show malignancy. Cervical cancer is one of the most treatable cancers if detected early, so women are urged to have annual or biannual Pap smear tests, and women who are rated II or higher should be tested even more frequently. Because they rely on the human eye for diagnosis, Pap tests are sometimes unreliable, but at this writing, no better affordable mode of testing exists.

25. (b) Uterine myomas are benign tumors often called fibroids that occur without symptoms in a surprisingly high percentage of women over 35 — perhaps as high as 25%. Women with fibroid tumors are usually encouraged to have biannual pelvic exams just to ensure that the tumors have not grown. Occasionally tumors may press against organs, cause heavy menstrual bleeding, or impede fertility, and in such cases a myomectomy to remove the fibroids may be performed.

26. (d) Hormones are the body's chemical messengers. They are produced by endocrine glands and move through the bloodstream to stimulate a particular action in some part of the body. Progesterone is manufactured by the corpus luteum, an endocrine tissue mass located in the ovary. It induces the changes in uterine mucus needed for the maintenance of pregnancy and helps initiate lactation.

27. (b) A typical menstrual cycle runs about 28 to 30 days. It begins with the first day of a menstrual period, which is followed approximately two weeks later by ovulation. An average period lasts four to six days. Much variation occurs in menstrual cycles; some women's cycles last 20 days, whereas others have 40-day cycles. An individual's cycle may vary with stress, age, travel, and pregnancy. A phenomenon often noted by women who live together is the gradual synchronization of cycles, so that all women in a household may end up regularly beginning their periods on the same day.

28. (a) At birth, a female baby holds about 400,000 eggs, or *ova*, in her ovaries. These are stored in immature form until puberty, when one ovum (sometimes more) will mature each month — from alternate ovaries — and will be released down the Fallopian tube to the uterus, to be fertilized or to disintegrate and be washed away during menstruation. If you are a woman, therefore, you contain at birth all the eggs you will ever produce.

29. (a) Except for the sex cells, all human cells contain 46 chromosomes arranged in 23 pairs. Egg cells contain 23 chromosomes, one of which is an X sex chromosome. Sperm cells contain 23 chromosomes, one of which is an X or Y sex chromosome. When an egg is fertilized, the resulting blastocyst contains the 23 chromosomes from the egg plus the 23 from the sperm for a total of 46. If an egg is fertilized by a sperm containing an X chromosome, the child will be a girl, XX. If the egg is fertilized by a sperm containing a Y chromosome, the child will be a boy, XY. Once the egg is fertilized, cells begin dividing to create new cells, some groups of which will be specially designed to manufacture the correct hormones, female or male. These hormones aid in the development of the appropriate sexual anatomy.

30. (c) As with all aspects of growth during puberty, the final result is predetermined by a woman's genetic code. Typically some initial breast growth takes place three or four years before the first menstruation, and adult size is reached within a year or two after the first menstruation. (Pregnancy and breastfeeding may cause later size changes.) Some women experience irregular growth; first one breast grows, then the other, and it is quite common to have breasts with size differences of a cup size or more. Exercise can shape breasts to some degree by expanding the underlying chest muscles, but the breasts themselves contain almost no muscle; they are made up primarily of fat cells and glandular tissue and therefore change shape with weight gain.

31. **(d)** Most women do not have sexual problems after a hysterectomy, but enough women do to make it an issue in postoperative care. Depression is often a cause of sexual dysfunction; women who have lost their ability to conceive may be depressed, whether they have lost it through surgery or through menopause. If the ovaries are removed (oophorectomy), reduced hormone levels can lead to loss of desire, and hormone therapy may be indicated. Rarely, when complications occur, nerve endings may be damaged in surgery, and this may block ordinary responses to stimulation. Many self-help groups exist for hysterectomy patients, and women may find that belonging to such organizations aids in their recuperation.

32. **(c)** PMS, or premenstrual syndrome, has only fairly recently been accepted as a true syndrome in certain women. A dip in hormone levels can lead to feelings of malaise and exhaustion. When muscles in the uterus contract to help expel the uterine lining in the menstrual fluid, sometimes an excess of prostaglandin can cause these contractions to become longer in duration and painful. Contractions may also take place in the intestines, leading to nausea. Bloating may be caused by the body's increased tendency to retain fluids at this time of the month, and the congestion of blood vessels may lead to a heavy, uncomfortable feeling. While no single therapy can completely cure the condition, women with unusually intense PMS may receive progesterone therapy.

33. **(d)** The cervix, from a word meaning "neck," is near the end of the vagina. Menstrual blood passes from the uterus through the cervix and out of the vagina. Unless blocked by a condom, diaphragm, or cervical cap, sperm move up the vagina and through the cervix to the uterus. In a woman who is not pregnant or has had no previous vaginal deliveries, the cervix is pink and firm, with a tiny hole in the center. In a pregnant woman, it is bluish and spongy. During childbirth, the cervix dilates to accommodate passage of the baby down the vagina.

34. **(d)** Estrogen is the hormone responsible for the menstrual cycle. During menopause, the ovaries no longer produce estrogen, and a sudden dip in hormone levels may lead to psychological and physical problems, including difficulty in absorbing calcium, which can lead to osteoporosis. Doctors may prescribe synthetic estrogen to counter these symptoms. Estrogen replacement therapy (ERT) is increasingly controversial, however, because links with breast and endometrial cancers have been found. Estrogen in varying amounts is also an ingredient in most birth control pills.

35. **(c)** The Bartholin's or vestibular glands are located on either side of the labia minora. With stimulation, they secrete a few drops of fluid. This fluid was once thought to be a lubricant for the vagina, but it is now clear that most lubrication actually occurs further up the vaginal passage. The purpose of Bartholin's glands' secretions is therefore unknown.

36. **(c)** People often wrongly believe that an intact hymen is a sign of virginity, and that the first act of intercourse must therefore involve pain and bleeding. The hymen is a membrane that stretches across the vaginal opening at birth, but begins to stretch and break down thereafter. A very few girls have a hymen at puberty that completely covers the vaginal opening, blocking menstrual flow, and these girls require minor surgery to correct the problem. The hymen can stretch to accomodate use of tampons, and in many cases, what remains of the hymen at the age of first intercourse is so minimal that no tearing or bleeding occurs.

37. (d) A D and C is used to treat uterine bleeding, incomplete abortion, and certain cancers. A standard pelvic exam is done by a gynecologist, general practitioner, or nurse, and involves a series of steps. Usually a woman undresses, puts on a gown, and lies on a table with her legs spread and bent at the knee and her feet in the "stirrups" at the end of the table. The doctor or nurse puts on gloves and checks the external pelvic area, looking for lice, unusual discharge, and irritations. Then he or she tells the patient to relax her pelvis and inserts a tool called the speculum into the vagina to hold the walls of the vagina apart and make visual examination easier. This part of the exam consists of a check for cervical and vaginal abnormalities. Swabs are used to take a Pap smear and a culture to check for gonorrhea or to test for chlamydia, herpes simplex virus (HSV), or vaginitis. Next the speculum is removed, and the doctor or nurse inserts two fingers into the vagina while keeping one hand on the patient's abdomen. This enables him or her to check for problems in the uterus, ovaries, and Fallopian tubes. The pelvic exam may also include a rectovaginal exam, in which the doctor or nurse inserts one finger in the rectum and one in the uterus.

38. (b) Toxic-shock syndrome, or TSS, is a bacterial infection caused by *Staphylococcus aureus*. Nearly three-fourths of the recent cases of the disease occurred in menstruating women who were using tampons, and the incidence was highest among teenage girls and women under 30. The warning signs include a sudden fever of 102° or higher, vomiting or diarrhea, a sunburn-like rash, dizziness or lightheadedness, and/or sore throat. The risk of TSS is lessened if you change tampons every four to six hours, use applicators rather than fingers to insert tampons, and/or alternate tampons with sanitary napkins. TSS has also been known to occur in women using diaphragms or cervical caps during their periods.

39. **(b)** It is worth remembering that although their numbers are small, women *have* become pregnant during their menstrual periods. Women with irregular or short cycles are particularly susceptible, but any woman who does not want a child should exercise as much caution at this time of month as she would at any other. Menstrual myths and taboos are difficult to overcome, but there is no evidence that horseback riding, swimming or bathing, or hard exercise of any kind can cause harm to a menstruating woman. Many women who were excused from gym class one week out of every month throughout their school careers find later that exercise actually alleviates cramps and makes them feel better rather than worse at this point in their cycle.

40. **(d)** A whole variety of glands and their hormones control standard operating procedures in the human female. The hypothalamus sends a message to the pituitary to start up the menstrual cycle. The pituitary then sends out two hormones: follicle-stimulating hormone (FSH), which stimulates the Graafian follicles in the ovaries to develop and the lining of the uterus to thicken; and luteinizing hormone (LH), which ripens one of the Graafian follicles to bursting point and thus begins an egg's journey down the Fallopian tube to the uterus. The burst follicle becomes the corpus luteum, which produces estrogen and progesterone. If fertilization does not take place, the corpus luteum dies, and estrogen and progesterone levels decline. Sensing this decline, the hypothalamus takes action and begins the cycle again. As a woman approaches menopause, her Graafian follicles occasionally fail to respond to hormonal stimulation. Some months they ripen; some months they do not. Failure of the follicles to ripen affects production of estrogen and progesterone. After a while, the follicles cannot respond at all. No eggs are released, menstruation no longer takes place, progesterone and nearly all estrogen cease to be produced, and conception is no longer possible.

TEST 2

What a Piece of Work: The Male Body

Men make love more intensely at twenty, but make love better, however, at thirty.

— CATHERINE THE GREAT

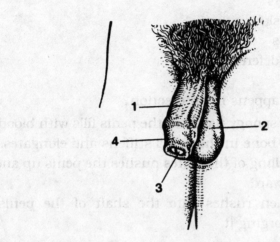

1. What is the part of the body labeled 1?

   a. penis

   b. bladder

   c. prostate

   d. testicle

2. What is the part of the body labeled 2?

   a. penis

   b. urethra

   c. scrotum

   d. epididymis

3. What is the part of the body labeled 3?

   a. urethra

   b. vas deferens

   c. glans

   d. testicle

4. What is the part of the body labeled 4?

   a. pubis

   b. foreskin

   c. anus

   d. vas deferens

5. What happens in an erection?

   a. The spongy tissue in the penis fills with blood.

   b. The bone in the penis stiffens and elongates.

   c. Swelling of the testes pushes the penis up and outward.

   d. Semen rushes into the shaft of the penis, engorging it.

6. What is the role of Cowper's glands in sexual activity?

   a. They release hormones into the bloodstream, causing rapid heartbeat and muscular tension.

   b. They secrete a small amount of fluid, which appears around the glans.

   c. They send a chemical message that tells the testes to send sperm to the urethra.

   d. They manufacture semen, which nourishes sperm.

7. About how many sperm are in an average ejaculation?

   a. 8,000

   b. 250,000

   c. 2 million

   d. 300 million

8. What is removed in circumcision?

   a. the scrotal sac

   b. the foreskin

   c. the foreskin and corona

   d. the tip of the glans

9. In order for a human baby to be born male,

   a. his mother's egg cell must contain a Y chromosome

   b. both father and mother must donate Y chromosomes

   c. his father's fertilizing sperm must contain a Y chromosome

   d. he must develop male sexual organs within the first month as a fetus

10. When does a boy's first erection usually take place?

   a. before birth

   b. at age 5 or 6

   c. while reading back issues of *National Geographic*

   d. at the onset of puberty

11. What is in the semen of an unsterilized man?

   a. spermatozoa and ova

   b. sperm and saline solution

   c. sperm and fluid from the prostate gland

   d. sperm and fluid from the ureter

12. What happens in a prostate exam?

   a. The doctor gently probes the patient's scrotum for lumps.

   b. The doctor inserts a finger in the patient's rectum and feels for the gland.

    c. The patient is asked to ejaculate into a flask or vial.

    d. all of the above

13. What is a nocturnal emission?

    a. the climax of a masturbatory fantasy

    b. an involuntary ejaculation during sleep

    c. the cycle of erections during REM sleep

    d. a release of fluid from the Cowper's glands

14. Why might an undescended testicle be dangerous?

    a. It puts a man at greater risk of testicular cancer.

    b. It may release sperm into the abdominal cavity.

    c. It can block operation of the bladder or kidneys.

    d. It could drop suddenly, dragging a man to the ground.

15. Which happens first as a boy reaches puberty?

    a. Sperm begin to be found in the ejaculate.

    b. Growth hormones initiate a growth spurt.

    c. Masturbation and nocturnal emissions increase.

    d. The testicles increase production of testosterone.

16. Which of these is *not* a typical sign of male development in the early stages of puberty?

    a. growth of the testicles

    b. growth of sparse facial hair

    c. shrinking of the larynx

    d. growth of the penis

17. Which of these is *not* a typical sign of male development in the later stages of puberty?

    a. growth of hair under arms

    b. growth of chest hair

    c. oily skin

    d. increased fluid in the scrotum

18. Which of the following compounds is a steroid?

    a. testosterone

    b. cholesterol

    c. cortisone

    d. all of the above

19. What physical changes take place during the period sometimes called the "male climacteric"?

    a. Erections take more time to achieve, and the time between ejaculation and the next erection is longer.

    b. The testicles descend into the scrotal sac, and the penis increases in length and width.

    c. The penis engorges, and sperm rush from the testicles to the vas deferens.

    d. Increased levels of testosterone cause the voice to deepen, muscles to expand, and hair to grow.

20. What is generally removed in the process of castration?

    a. the scrotal sac

    b. the penis

    c. the testicles

    d. the will to live

21. Which of these is most likely to cause impotence?

    a. high blood pressure

    b. excessive weight loss

    c. frequent masturbation

    d. all of the above

22. What is the average length of a man's erect penis?

    a. 3 inches

    b. 10 inches

    c. 6 inches

    d. 8 inches

23. How many erections will an average, healthy male achieve during a night's sleep?

    a. 12

    b. 8

    c. 5

    d. 1

24. What happens to a sufferer of Peyronie's disease?

    a. He becomes infertile.

    b. His penis curves upward on erection.

    c. He cannot ejaculate.

    d. His penis develops a precancerous lesion.

25. Why do doctors often advise men with low sperm counts to wear boxer shorts?

    a. to allow oxygen to circulate in the penis

    b. to improve blood circulation in the sexual organs

    c. to lower the body temperature in the testicles

    d. to encourage spontaneous erections

26. In a physical examination, why do doctors perform a "cough test"?

    a. to detect a hernia in the scrotum

    b. to check the flow of blood in the penis

    c. to determine if the testicles are properly descended

    d. to feel for cancerous lumps

27. What happens when a male child is born with an extra X chromosome?

    a. He develops a vagina and ovaries.

    b. He becomes aggressive and hostile.

    c. He is able to bear a child.

    d. He develops breasts and is infertile.

28. Which of these is a common cause of baldness?

    a. frequent sexual activity

    b. masturbation

    c. genetic predisposition

    d. excessive testosterone

29. Which of these is an effect of the hormone testosterone?

    a. development of sexual desire

    b. maintenance of blood pressure

    c. development of spermatozoa

    d. rude whistling at passing women

30. Which of these doctors should a man visit for problems of the reproductive tract?

    a. a gynecologist

    b. a urologist

    c. a neurologist

    d. a hematologist

31. Why is mumps a dangerous disease for post-pubertal men to develop?

    a. It can result in impotence.

    b. The virus interacts with testosterone and can be fatal.

    c. It can be transmitted to women during sexual intercourse.

    d. It can attack the testicle and leave it sterile.

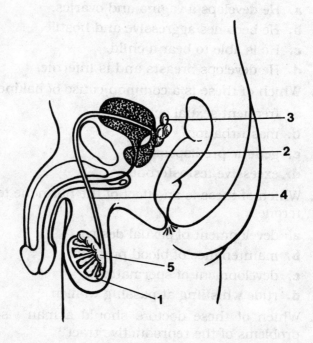

32. What is the part of the body labeled 5?
   a. urethra
   b. prostate gland
   c. epididymis
   d. vas deferens

33. What is the part of the body labeled 4?
   a. testis
   b. vas deferens
   c. seminal vesicle
   d. epididymis

34. What is the part of the body labeled 1?

    a. prostate

    b. seminal vesicle

    c. urethra

    d. testis

35. What is the role of the body part labeled 2?

    a. It secretes fluid that helps sperm grow.

    b. It protects the testicles.

    c. It regulates the flow of sperm during ejaculation.

    d. It regulates erection.

36. What is the role of the body part labeled 3?

    a. It stores the hormone testosterone.

    b. It stores the sperm and produces fructose.

    c. It regulates urine flow.

    d. It is a vestigial organ.

37. What happens in the disease priapism?

    a. The sufferer cannot ejaculate.

    b. The penis grows too large to fit in a woman's vagina.

    c. The sufferer cannot urinate.

    d. The penis remains erect, even without desire.

38. What common effect does a varicocele have?

    a. impotence

    b. low sperm count

    c. pain on ejaculation

    d. inability to ejaculate

39. Which of these is used by doctors to treat impotence?

    a. yohimbine (made from the bark of an African tree)

    b. powdered rhinoceros horn

    c. Orgatron–12 (made from a Mexican plant)

    d. all of the above

40. What role does the urethra play in male sexuality?

    a. It carries the semen that later mixes with sperm.

    b. It contains the blood that produces an erection.

    c. The ejaculate moves through it and out the tip of the penis.

    d. The urethra is only involved in urination.

TEST 2: Explanatory Answers

1. **(a)** The penis is the main male sex organ. In addition to its sexual function, it is used for urination. It is made up of a head and shaft, and in humans, it contains spongy tissue, blood vessels, and nerves.

2. **(c)** The scrotum is a soft, two-part sac that contains the testicles. It acts as a temperature control for the sperm-producing testicles, making sure that they are kept at an ideal temperature; that is, slightly below body temperature. The scrotum responds automatically to external changes in temperature by contracting, drawing the testicles nearer to the body, or relaxing, and moving them away from the body.

3. **(c)** The head of the penis is called the glans. It contains many nerve endings and is the most sensitive part of the penis. The frenulum is an especially sensitive area located under the penis where the shaft and head of the penis meet.

4. **(b)** The prepuce or foreskin is a retractable hood of skin that covers the head of the penis of an uncircumcised man. A similar hood covers a woman's clitoris.

5. **(a)** The right physical or mental stimulation causes blood to rush to the corpus cavernosum and the corpus spongiosum, areas of spongy tissue along the penis. The entire process can take a few seconds, but as men age, it often takes longer and requires more direct stimulation. In young men, the erect penis often points upward, but many men's erections point straight out or downward. A slight curve in the erect penis is not unusual.

6. **(b)** Cowper's glands are located under the prostate, one on either side of the urethra. As a man becomes sexually aroused, the glands secrete a small amount of clear lubricating fluid, which moves down the urethra and appears on the glans. Despite the fact that this happens before ejaculation, the fluid usually contains some sperm and is therefore potentially a cause of pregnancy.

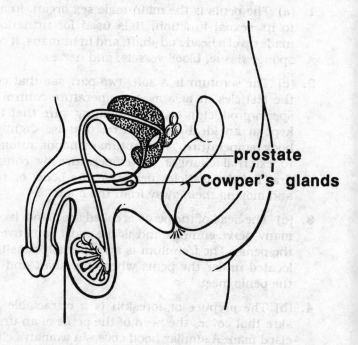

prostate

Cowper's glands

7. **(d)** Biologically designed to provide the highest possible probability of impregnation, the average ejaculation is about a teaspoonful of semen, containing a whopping 200 to 400 million sperm. Sperm count is very susceptible to environment, however, and a man who is in poor health or has had a recent fever may have a significantly lower count. The ingestion of various drugs, including marijuana, can also lower sperm count. Sperm counts can be reduced or eliminated, moreover, by obstructions in the vas deferens or ejaculatory duct, by undescended testicles, or by swollen veins in the scrotum, among other causes.

8. **(b)** Circumcision as a religious and cultural ritual has been around for centuries and will be discussed in more detail in Test 8. Nowadays this optional operation generally takes place shortly after birth. It consists of removal of the foreskin, or prepuce, the fold of skin

that covers the glans. There is some medical evidence that circumcision may reduce the risk of certain cancers and infections, probably due to the fact that smegma, a glandular secretion, cannot build up on a circumcised penis. Occasionally circumcision is performed later in life if a man has difficulty retracting his foreskin during urination or sexual activity.

9. **(c)** An egg cell contains one sex chromosome, an X. A sperm cell may contain an X or a Y sex chromosome, and it is the sperm's sex chromosome that determines the sex of a baby. If the egg is fertilized by a sperm containing a Y chromosome, the resulting baby will have one X and one Y chromosome, and will therefore be a boy.

10. **(a)** Boys are often born with erect penises, and the cycle of erections that marks a healthy boy begins in the womb. At this stage and immediately after birth, the response is strictly involuntary, as it is through adulthood during REM sleep. It does not take babies long, however, to learn that touch can cause pleasurable feelings and lead to an erection.

11. **(c)** Sperm are manufactured in the testes and stored near the seminal vesicles (see the diagram on page 44). At ejaculation, the vesicles release a fluid that activates the sperm, and this is added to a milky fluid from the prostate gland. Semen is designed to give nourishment to the sperm during their trip up the vagina. A man who has had a vasectomy ejaculates semen without any sperm because the pathway from the testicles to the seminal vesicles has been blocked.

12. **(b)** The prostate gland surrounds the urethra (see the diagram on page 44). Cancer of the prostate is the third leading cancer-related cause of death in men. Problems with the prostate often affect the urinary tract, with symptoms including painful urination, blood in the urine, and difficulty urinating. Often the problem is caused by a benign enlargement of the gland; over half

of men over 50 have some enlargement. Cancer and enlargement of the prostate can be detected early by a medical exam, and all men over 40 should have the exam once a year. In the exam, the patient bends at the waist, and the doctor inserts a gloved finger into the anus and probes the gland through the wall of the rectum. The doctor feels for lumps or distension and then examines the glans of the penis for any discharge caused by the probing of the gland.

13. **(b)** Kinsey once reported that four out of five men had experienced nocturnal emissions, or "wet dreams." Some emissions seem to be tied to erotic dreams, but others have no obvious sexual basis at all. Young boys just entering puberty are often alarmed and confused by their first nocturnal emissions, but wet dreams seem simply to be a part of natural behavior. Many women (perhaps two out of five) experience nocturnal orgasms as well.

14. **(a)** During the first months of its existence, a fetus's sex glands are in its abdomen. They slowly migrate downward toward the pelvis, where, in a girl, the ovaries stop. In a boy, the glands continue to descend, emerging in the scrotum between the fourth and fifth months of pregnancy. In a small percentage of cases, a boy is born with one or both testicles still in the lower abdomen. When this happens, the warmth of the body prevents sperm from being produced. In addition, the risk of cancer in the testicles increases dramatically. For these reasons, surgery, or more rarely, hormonal therapy, may be recommended to move the testicles into the scrotum.

15. **(d)** Testosterone is responsible for nearly all of the external changes that take place in a boy as he goes through puberty. The age of boys at this beginning stage of puberty ranges all the way from preteen to midteen.

16. **(c)** The larynx, like most internal and external body parts, enlarges during puberty, causing a boy's voice to deepen. Other early signs of puberty may include sparse pubic and underarm hair and a boy's first ejaculation.

17. **(d)** Fluid in the scrotum is a sign of a condition called hydrocele, which in some cases requires surgical correction. Besides having occasional acne and continued growth of hair, a boy in the late stages of puberty will often achieve his adult height and muscle mass.

18. **(d)** Steroids are a type of organic compound containing four linked hydrocarbon rings. All hormones are made either from protein or steroid. The group of hormones made from steroid includes testosterone, estrogen, progesterone, and cortisone, among others. The steroids taken by athletes are generally synthetic testosterone. These steroids increase muscle bulk while at the same time shrinking the sex glands. There is evidence that long-term use of such steroids can permanently damage normal development of bones and muscles, can cause sexual dysfunction, may lead to manic behavior and even psychosis, and may cause prostate cancer. It's hard to imagine that the urge to run faster and jump higher is worth the risk.

19. **(a)** Unlike the female climacteric (menopause), in men the climacteric does not have a specific biological marker; i.e., cessation of menses, hot flashes, etc. With age, testosterone levels decrease, leading in late middle age to a slowing down of sexual responses. Some men in their 50s and 60s will find it more difficult and time-consuming to achieve an erection than in their younger days, and they may find their orgasms less intense. It may take far longer than before for them to achieve a second erection after ejaculation. All of these manifestations are normal. Some men find that an increased ability to maintain an erection once it is achieved enhances their sex lives and that of their partners.

However, as with some women reaching menopause, some men may feel deeply depressed during this time and pass through what some call a "mid-life crisis."

20. **(c)** Today we define "castration" as the removal of the testicles. If the testicles are removed before a boy reaches puberty, he will lack the secondary sex characteristics of a man due to the loss of his producers of testosterone. If the operation takes place later in life, loss of testosterone will cause a reduction in sex drive as well as degeneration of certain secondary sex characteristics. Today, postoperative hormone therapy may be used for a patient who loses testicles to cancer, and it is now possible for such a patient to have a penile implant to retain the ability to have erections. Testicle implants for cosmetic purposes are also common. Of course, a man without testicles cannot impregnate a woman; he has lost the ability to manufacture sperm. Sigmund Freud got a lot of mileage out of his "castration anxiety" theories; when he referred to castration, he meant the removal of the penis.

21. **(a)** While impotence, the inability to achieve or maintain an erection, can occur at almost any time and for many reasons, the most frequent physiological cause is impaired blood flow. High blood pressure can interfere with blood flow, and many drugs that control high blood pressure can also cause impotence. Other common physiological factors in impotence include testosterone deficiency, nerve damage, diabetes, and prescription or recreational drug use. Stress, fear of failure, and other psychological factors can also cause impotence.

22. **(c)** An average erection is 6 inches in length, and an average flaccid penis has a length of 3 to 6 inches. However, a range from 4½ to 8 inches for an erect penis is common, and smaller or larger penis sizes do not impair sexual satisfaction for either men or women.

23. **(c)** Most nocturnal erections occur during REM (rapid eye movement) sleep and last about half an hour. These

erections do not always lead to nocturnal emissions; they are not necessarily linked to sexual thoughts and dreams but may just be reactions to electrical impulses from the brain. Often a man will be unaware of all except the last erection, which is evident when he awakens. The number of nocturnal erections usually lessens with age.

24. **(b)** In Peyronie's disease, named after the eighteenth century French doctor François de la Peyronie, the erect penis develops an upward curve of 10 to more than 90 degrees. The condition is the result of a buildup of scar tissue, and is sometimes associated with moderate alcohol intake or use of beta blockers. In most cases, however, researchers still do not know why this condition occurs. It can make erection painful and can be corrected with surgery, but in one third of sufferers, it disappears spontaneously.

25. **(c)** The testicles are intended to hang loosely from the body, keeping their temperature at four degrees Fahrenheit below body temperature. Tight shorts compress the testicles, warming them, and can lead to a lowered sperm count.

26. **(a)** An indirect inguinal hernia occurs when the intestine protrudes into the scrotal sac. It can be caused by weakening of the abdominal wall due to age or by sudden or intense physical exertion. In the "cough test," the doctor pushes the scrotal sac toward the abdomen as the patient coughs, and feels for a hernial bulge. A hernia can only be corrected with surgery, but use of a truss can keep a non-strangulated hernia (one whose blood supply has not been cut off) from worsening.

27. **(d)** Klinefelter's syndrome, in which a male has 47 chromosomes with an extra X chromosome, affects 0.14 to 0.25% of men. These men do not produce sperm, have small testicles and penis, and experience abnormal growth of breast tissue. Another chromosomal disorder, the 47 XYY syndrome, gives an extra Y chromosome and affects 0.1 to 0.2% of men. These men are often fertile, but may have trouble controlling their impulses.

28. (c) Male pattern baldness, apparent in 50% of men by age 45, is an inherited condition and leads to gradual hair loss from the temples back. The drug Rogaine has helped some men to halt or slow hair loss, but only hair transplants can reverse the balding process.

29. (a) Testosterone, often called the "male sex hormone," is produced by the Leydig's cells in the testes. It helps to develop the changes apparent in puberty — growth of body hair, muscle and bone size, development of sexual organs, stimulation of spermatozoa, and development of the libido. Answers b and c refer to hydrocortisone, made by the adrenal gland, follicle-stimulating hormone, made by the pituitary gland; and thyroid

30. (b) While a family practice doctor or an internist can treat general problems relating to most body parts, a specialist in the male reproductive tract is called a urologist. The other doctors mentioned are specialists of the female reproductive tract, of the nervous system, and of the blood.

31. (d) Mumps, usually a childhood viral infection of the salivary glands, can occur in the testicles after puberty. It causes intensely painful swelling, which may leave the testicle inoperative. However, adult mumps will usually attack only one testicle.

32. (c) The epididymis is shaped like a comma and is located at the back of the testicle. It is filled with tiny tubes in which sperm grow to maturity, a process taking about three months. The sperm from the tail of the epididymis are fully mature, while those in the head do not yet have the ability to swim.

33. (b) The vas deferens is the tube through which the sperm move when they leave the epididymis. It is over 12 inches long and is mostly muscle.

34. (d) The testis contains the Leydig's cells, which make testosterone, and the cells that manufacture sperm. It also includes cells called Sertoli cells, which provide nourishment for the developing sperm.

35. (a) The prostate gland manufactures nutrients that keep sperm alive on their journey from the epididymis downward. It provides more than one quarter of the fluid in the ejaculate. The prostate is especially prone to infection and can be the site of cancer development or benign enlargement.

36. (b) The seminal vesicles are located directly above and on either side of the prostate gland. Their role is to manufacture the fructose-based semen, the main nourishment for sperm. This sugary substance contains approximately six calories per ejaculation.

37. (d) Priapism is named after the Greek god of fertility, Priapus, who reputedly had a huge penis. In priapism, blood is unable to drain from the penis, resulting in permanent, painful erection. The condition can develop spontaneously; when it has a known cause, it is often linked with diseases of the red blood cells or spinal injuries. If the disease is not treated quickly, the blood clots, and scarring ensues. The condition often results in impotence.

38. (b) A varicocele is a collection of varicose veins in the testicle, usually on the left side. The varicocele, felt as a lump in the scrotum, can be symptomless, but it can cause discomfort and infertility linked to low sperm count.

39. (a) Yohimbine hydrochloride is a drug that has been approved by the FDA for treating blood-pressure problems, but not for treating impotence. According to Dr. Yosh Taguchi, however, it helps 20 to 30 % of men with mild impotence, and works by blocking the flow of blood from blood vessels. Injections of papaverine, also not FDA-approved, into the penis, and inflatable or semirigid penile implants are treatments with greater success rates. Powdered rhinoceros horn is reputed (falsely so) to be an aphrodisiac, and Orgatron–12 is a compound offered by mail-order houses that has no known beneficial effect on impotence.

40. (c) Both urine and ejaculatory fluid move through the urethra on their way out of the body. A valve at the base of the bladder closes prior to ejaculation, preventing urine from flowing. Glands near the urethra release fluid that cleans the tube and neutralizes its acidity, preparing the canal for sperm.

The Big O: Human Sexuality

Why Don't We Do It in the Road?

— *JOHN LENNON & PAUL McCARTNEY*

1. Which of the following occurs in the arousal phase of male sexual response?

   a. The male begins to fantasize.

   b. He ejaculates.

   c. His blood pressure rises.

   d. His bladder opening closes.

2. Which of the following might occur in the plateau phase of male sexual response?

   a. The Cowper's glands produce fluid.

   b. The body returns to its prearoused state.

   c. Ejaculation takes place.

   d. Momentary loss of consciousness may occur.

3. What occurs during the orgasm phase of male sexual response?

   a. The seminal vesicles, anus, and urethra contract.

   b. The penis pulls back toward the body and shrinks in size.

   c. The testicles rotate.

   d. all of the above

4. Which of the following does *not* occur in the resolution phase of male sexual response?

   a. Blood drains from the genitals.

   b. The bladder opening closes.

   c. The male often falls asleep.

   d. The heart rate slows.

5. At what moment is loss of virginity commonly thought to occur?

    a. when the hymen is broken

    b. when the first orgasm occurs

    c. during the first incidence of masturbation

    d. when sexual penetration occurs

6. Which of the following is *not* a cause of premature ejaculation?

    a. previous practice of withdrawal as birth control

    b. previous masturbation to a quick climax

    c. early sexual experience with a prostitute

    d. the presence of a foreskin

7. What is dyspareunia?

    a. retarded ejaculation

    b. painful intercourse

    c. insufficient vaginal lubrication

    d. an infectious condition of the cervix

8. In butch-femme lesbianism,

    a. one partner pretends to be a man

    b. one partner is passive and the other is aggressive

    c. both partners wear short haircuts and masculine clothes

    d. one partner is bisexual

9. Which of the following sexual aids can be helpful in restoring potency?

    a. Spanish fly

    b. amyl nitrate

    c. penile rings

    d. ginseng

10. Where is the G-spot reputedly located?

    a. inside the vagina

    b. between the clitoris and the vagina

    c. on the glans

    d. behind the testicles

11. What is the practice of cunnilingus?

    a. oral stimulation of a man's genitals

    b. oral stimulation of a woman's genitals

    c. anal intercourse

    d. manual stimulation of a woman's genitals

12. Which of these most closely defines celibacy?

    a. devoting oneself to religion

    b. refusing to have oral sex

    c. refraining from sexual activity

    d. remaining a virgin

13. What is tribadism?

    a. genital stimulation by rubbing

    b. sex with three participants

    c. anal intercourse

    d. oral intercourse among men

14. What percentage of the population of the United States is bisexual?

    a. 1%

    b. 5 to 8%

    c. 10 to 15%

    d. 20%

15. The average number of times per week couples in their 20s or 30s have sexual intercourse is

a. either not enough, or too much

b. 2 to 3

c. 4 to 5

d. 7 to 8

16. What is a transvestite?

a. a person who dresses as one of the opposite sex

b. a person whose external genitalia are ambiguous

c. a person whose gender identity is that of the opposite sex

d. a person who possesses both male and female genitalia

17. Which of the following is true of male masturbation?

a. It can cause the penis to grow longer.

b. It can cause skin problems.

c. It can cause the penis to curve.

d. none of the above

18. Should a healthy woman refrain from having intercourse while she is menstruating?

a. yes, during the days when the flow is heaviest

b. no, not at all

c. yes, during the entire period

d. no, as long as her partner wears a condom

19. Which of the following has aphrodisiac effects?

   a. strychnine
   b. chocolate
   c. prairie oysters
   d. sarsaparilla

20. What occurs when a couple engages in "69"?

   a. They try 69 different positions of lovemaking over a period of several months.
   b. They perform oral sex on one another at the same time.
   c. One partner massages the other partner.
   d. A third party is introduced into the sexual act.

21. Which of the following is *not* a true statement about fellatio?

   a. Some states have laws against this practice.
   b. A majority of married heterosexual couples have engaged in this practice.
   c. A majority of gay male couples have engaged in this practice.
   d. Fellatio often refers to mutual masturbation.

22. What is primary orgasmic dysfunction in women?

   a. the inability to reach orgasm during intercourse
   b. the inability to reach orgasm by any means
   c. the inability to reach orgasm in a heterosexual encounter
   d. the inability to reach orgasm with one's primary partner

23. Sex researchers and therapists believe that the main role of sexual fantasy is to

    a. allow people to discuss their socially unacceptable sexual desires

    b. enable the id to split off from the ego and act on its aggressive or masochistic impulses

    c. provide a safe outlet for sexual curiosity

    d. all of the above

24. About what percentage of the total adult population is homosexual?

    a. 10%

    b. 5%

    c. 2%

    d. less than 2%

25. Which of these statements about sexual positions for heterosexuals is *not* true?

    a. "Rear entry" refers to anal intercourse.

    b. The "woman on top" position has been popular for centuries.

    c. The missionary position is the one used most often in the United States.

    d. Certain positions are better than others if a couple is trying to conceive.

26. Which of the following is *not* a normal part of foreplay?

    a. kissing

    b. breast manipulation

    c. oral-genital stimulation

    d. intercourse

27. What is vasocongestion?
   a. a rush of blood to the genital area
   b. a buildup of vaseline on a battery-operated sex toy
   c. constriction of the muscles around the vagina
   d. swelling of the mucus plug at the cervical opening

28. If a woman reaches the plateau stage of sexual arousal,
   a. she has missed her chance to have an orgasm
   b. continued stimulation can lead to orgasm
   c. her blood pressure slowly returns to normal
   d. her muscles contract as many as 15 times

29. What is always true of a female orgasm?
   a. It involves contractions of both the vagina and uterus.
   b. It involves contractions of the vagina only.
   c. It involves a single muscle contraction, but multiple orgasm may lead to additional contractions.
   d. It involves ejaculation of fluid from the urethra.

30. What is the difference between the resolution phases of sexual excitement in men and in women?
   a. Women take significantly longer to return to normal pulse and breathing rates.
   b. Men take significantly longer to return to normal pulse and breathing rates.
   c. At the beginning of resolution, women can return to plateau and orgasm; most men cannot.
   d. At the beginning of resolution, men can return to plateau and orgasm; women cannot.

31. What is the age at which humans reach their so-called "sexual peak"?

   a. late teens for men; late 30s for women

   b. early 20s for men and women

   c. late 20s for men; early 40s for women

   d. late teens for men; early 20s for women

32. Women who masturbate are *least* likely to

   a. use their hands

   b. stroke their genital areas

   c. insert objects into their vaginas

   d. rub against something

33. What is multiple orgasm?

   a. return to orgasm from the resolution phase of sexual arousal

   b. female orgasm involving rapid pulsations in the vagina

   c. orgasm by more than one method of arousal

   d. the goal of group sex

34. Who is a likely candidate for a sex change operation?

   a. a homosexual

   b. a transvestite

   c. a hermaphrodite

   d. a transsexual

35. Anal intercourse is a feasible means of preventing

   a. sexually transmitted diseases

   b. infections

   c. pregnancy

   d. AIDS

36. Which term from the Latin is *not* matched correctly with its translation?

   a. *cunnilingus*: "one who licks the vulva"

   b. *fellatio*: "sucking"

   c. *coitus*: "desire or lust"

   d. *pudendum*: "shameful thing"

37. What is hypersexuality?

   a. the equal ability to achieve satisfaction with either a male or a female partner

   b. an uncontrollable and unsatisfying need for sex

   c. sex with a speed freak

   d. the appearance at puberty of both male and female secondary sex characteristics

38. Penile implants are occasionally prescribed for men who

   a. do not manufacture sperm

   b. cannot maintain an erection

   c. have one undescended testicle

   d. all of the above

39. According to the Kinsey Report, nearly half of all people who request sex therapy are diagnosed as having problems with

   a. impotence

   b. inability to achieve orgasm

   c. infertility

   d. lack of desire

40. Someone who is heterosexist

a. sees sex between men and women as the only valid sexual option

b. objects to sexual relations between people of different races

c. has a negative attitude toward heterosexuality

d. enjoys interspecies sex

TEST 3: Explanatory Answers

1. **(c)** The Masters and Johnson model of human sexual response defines four distinct phases. The first is the arousal, or excitement, phase. As a man becomes mentally aroused — whether by sexual activity or sexual thoughts — his blood pressure rises, his heart beats faster, and his skin becomes more sensitive. Blood flows to his genitals, causing his penis to become erect and his testicles to pull in closer to his body.

2. **(a)** As a man moves from arousal to plateau, muscular tension grows, a rashlike flush might appear, and the size of the glans and testicles might increase. Often, the Cowper's glands produce pre-ejaculatory fluid, a drop or two of which might leave the penis.

3. **(a)** In an orgasm, which lasts only seconds, a man's seminal vesicles and prostate contract, forcing the ejaculate into the urethra. Then the penis and urethra contract, and ejaculation occurs. These rhythmic contractions can be accompanied by facial grimaces and involuntary sounds.

4. **(b)** In the resolution phase, which follows orgasm, the body slowly returns to its normal state. Blood pressure drops, and blood leaves the penis and other organs. Breathing and heart rate slow down. Most men need a period of time — from several minutes to days — before they can achieve another orgasm, but a recent study documented in *The Kinsey Institute New Report on Sex* suggests that some men are able to experience multiple orgasms and ejaculations without loss of erection.

5. **(d)** Although the definition of virginity can differ from culture to culture, and even from person to person, a virgin is usually considered to be someone who has not had sexual intercourse. The definition has historically had more importance for women than for men, as virginity was linked with a woman's honor and, by extension, with the honor of her family.

6. **(d)** Masters and Johnson describe a premature ejaculator as a man whose lack of control of his ejaculation

leads to a failure to satisfy his partner in at least 50% of coital experiences. Often, premature ejaculation is the result of an ingrained habit of quick ejaculation when masturbating, having early sexual relations with a prostitute, or using withdrawal as a method of contraception (the last two being potential sources of anxiety). The best treatment for this problem is sex therapy, in which the partner is taught to squeeze the erect penis, reducing the desire to ejaculate. The man is then stimulated to near orgasm, and again the "squeeze technique" is used. This procedure may continue for up to 20 minutes before ejaculation is allowed. Eventually, use of the squeeze technique aids most men in prolonging the sexual act.

7. **(b)** Painful intercourse, or dyspareunia, can affect either men or women. According to the Kinsey Report, about half of the reported cases result from feelings of fear or guilt about sex, or inadequate information on foreplay and arousal techniques. Other causes include infections of the reproductive tract in both sexes, and in women vaginitis, vaginal atrophy, gonorrhea, ovarian cysts, or endometriosis. The pain may occur in women either at the vaginal opening or deep inside the vagina.

8. **(b)** Butch-femme lesbianism, which was more popular before the Gay Liberation movements of the 1960s than it is now, is a relationship in which one partner is passive and receptive and the other is aggressive. While some feminist lesbians criticize this form of role-playing, which they claim is modeled on heterosexual behavior and is sexist, advocates state that the roles are valid ways to explore female sexuality.

9. **(c)** The penile ring, or "cock ring," fits on the base of the penis and retains blood in the organ, helping to maintain an erection. However, when used improperly, the ring can damage the urethra or blood vessels in the penis, making erection without the ring even more difficult.

10. **(a)** The G-spot, named after German gynecologist Ernest Gräfenberg, is supposedly found about two inches inside the vagina. It is said to be a small mass of tissue that is very sensitive to stimulation; when stimulated, it supposedly contributes to an "ejaculation" of fluid from the urethra (it is unclear what this fluid is, or even if it exists). The G-spot's existence has not been proved; if accepted, some feminists fear it could reintroduce the debunked ideal of the vaginal orgasm, leading to feelings of inadequacy among women who need direct clitoral stimulation to reach climax.

11. **(b)** Cunnilingus, or oral stimulation of a woman's genitals, can be used as a part of foreplay or as a means to bring a woman to orgasm. While some cultures pronounce the practice taboo, and some individuals are shocked or offended by it, many women feel that it makes orgasm especially pleasurable and easy to achieve.

12. **(c)** Celibacy can have different meanings for different people, but in general it indicates a choice to refrain from sexual activity. This may or may not include masturbation. Some people become celibate out of religious beliefs; others simply choose to take a break from sex to give themselves time to rechannel their emotional energy. Still others have celibacy thrust upon them — after the breakup of a relationship, for example.

13. **(a)** Stimulation of the genitals by rubbing is one form of lesbian sexual activity; heterosexuals can become aroused this way as well. Lesbians also practice cunnilingus and penetration with fingers or hands. Occasionally — less often than is generally assumed — a dildo, or phallus-shaped item, is used.

14. **(c)** When bisexuality is defined as having sexual activity with both sexes over a period of several years, then 10 to 15% of the population conforms to that definition. The Kinsey scale of sexual orientation, developed in the late 1940s, rates sexual orientation from 0 (exclusively heterosexual) to 6 (exclusively homosexual). From the

Kinsey Institute's research, it is clear that many people fall into the region between these two extremes. Sigmund Freud believed that all humans are born with a potential for being bisexual; his and others' studies postulate that sexual orientation in many is fluid and can shift depending on emotional, social, and environmental factors.

15. **(b)** While the statistical average for weekly sexual activity is 2 to 3 times for a couple in their twenties or thirties, many couples have sex much more or less frequently. Frequency of sexual relations tends to lessen as age increases, but again this is an average; individuals may have very different experiences. The key factor in determining frequency of intercourse for a couple is balancing the desires of both partners.

16. **(a)** Transvestites are people who must dress as one of the other sex to achieve full sexual satisfaction. They differ from cross dressers in that cross dressers only dress as the other sex to stimulate desire and may be able to achieve sexual satisfaction without that stimulation. The other conditions mentioned are intersexuality, transsexuality, and hermaphroditism.

17. **(d)** Myths about masturbation continue to proliferate, but facts are harder to pin down. According to Alfred Kinsey's early research, 94% of all men have masturbated at some time during their lives. The practice does not change the shape or size of the penis, cause illness, or influence later sexuality, although it is possible that rapid masturbatory orgasm can lead to premature ejaculation. Even when in a relationship, many men continue to masturbate, finding self-stimulation a way to supplement partner-oriented sexual activity.

18. **(b)** Though many cultures have taboos against sex during menstruation, the only time that this practice is not advisable is when the woman is HIV positive, or has antibodies to the AIDS virus, making transmission of the virus to her partner more likely. (A woman who is HIV positive should have her partner wear a condom during every act of intercourse.) Many women have found that orgasm can help to relieve menstrual cramps, but others prefer to abstain from sex during menstruation.

19. (a) While all of the substances noted have at one time or another been reputed to be aphrodisiacs, only strychnine has the ability to heighten sensitivity to physical stimulation. However, it is also a lethal poison; one is more likely to die than to have a heightened orgasm after ingestion. Chocolate was once thought to be so powerful an aphrodisiac that monks were forbidden to eat it. Prairie oysters, or bull testicles, were reputed to impart great virility, and sarsaparilla, thought to contain a chemical similar to testosterone, is a popular soft-drink flavoring.

20. (b) Sixty-nine is so named because the couple lies in the configuration of a 6 and a 9 in order to perform oral sex on one another at the same time.

21. (d) Fellatio is the name for oral sex that involves oral stimulation of the penis. It is the sexual practice most commonly used by gay male couples, but studies show a majority of married heterosexual couples have tried it as well. It is one of three practices condemned by sodomy laws in some states; this will be discussed in more detail in Test 7.

22. (b) Masters and Johnson isolated two basic types of orgasmic dysfunctions in women. A woman with "primary orgasmic dysfunction" has never achieved orgasm by any means, except perhaps in her sleep. Other nonorgasmic women are "situationally nonorgasmic" and have reached orgasm at some point in their lifetimes; this orgasm may have come about through masturbation, oral sex or manual stimulation with a male or female partner, or intercourse. Some can reach orgasm only through masturbation, some only through coitus but not through masturbation, and some can achieve orgasm on rare, seemingly random occasions. Masters and Johnson developed a multi-step sex therapy system for dealing with these dysfunctions, relying on communication and slow-paced "sensate-focus" exercises. Couples are encouraged to give and receive sensual (but not necessarily sexual) pleasure to learn what feels good to them both. Occasionally, men are nonorgasmic as well, a dysfunction sometimes termed "retarded ejaculation." Usually such men can ejaculate during masturbation or oral sex, but maintain an erection without ejaculating during intercourse.

23. **(c)** Although some people would indeed like to act out their sexual fantasies, most are content to fantasize in seclusion and in safety. Fantasy allows people to explore their own arousal; many people use tried-and-true fantasies to arouse themselves during masturbation or sex with a partner. Many people daydream about sexual encounters they would like to have, perhaps with unattainable figures such as movie stars; just as many fantasize about encounters they would never want to have come true — sado-masochistic relationships, sex with family members, or group sex are all examples of common fantasies.

24. **(a)** According to demographic studies done by the Kinsey Institute, about 7% of adult females and 13% of adult males consider themselves homosexual. Many more adults have had homosexual experiences but consider themselves primarily heterosexual. When Kinsey himself first reported on this in the 1950s, he received a great deal of criticism from people who could not accept such a high figure. Now the figure is considered by some to be unrealistically low.

25. **(a)** There are a variety of possible sexual positions for heterosexual intercourse, and according to art and written records, most if not all have been around throughout recorded history. The popularity of a given position depends on cultural biases as well as personal preference. In the United States, the missionary position (man on top, face-to-face) is the most common, but as the name indicates, other cultures prefer other positions. (The position supposedly got its name from South Sea islanders surprised by the "strange" sexual practices of white Christian missionaries.) Two other common positions are "woman on top," which affords more control to the woman and therefore is often recommended for nonorgasmic women and men with problems of premature ejaculation, who can remain relatively still in this position; and "rear entry," in which the penis enters the vagina when the woman's back is to the man. Positions that allow the semen to linger in the vagina and not run out are considered best for couples trying to conceive, but intercourse in *any* position (yes, *including* standing up) may lead to pregnancy if the couple is fertile.

26. (d) As its name indicates, foreplay is that sexual activity that comes before the main event, usually considered to be intercourse. However, foreplay can often and quite normally be an end in itself, whether or not it leads to orgasm.

27. (a) One of the primary indicators that a person is in the excitement stage of sexual activity is the rush of blood to the genitals. In a man, this causes erection; in a woman, it leads to lubrication of the vagina as the increased blood flow pushes tissue fluid through the vaginal walls and also darkens the color of the labia. Other external signs of excitement in women include nipple erection, swelling of the clitoris, and, in some women, a rashlike patch known as a sex flush. Other internal changes include expansion of the vagina. Increased blood pressure and pulse rate are evident in both men and women.

28. (b) The plateau stage, as defined by Masters and Johnson, is the stage of arousal at which tension is highest and orgasm is likely. The back of the vagina swells, lifting the cervix and uterus, while the opening of the vagina narrows. Continued stimulation is likely to cause orgasm, but many women reach the plateau stage and go no further.

29. **(a)** Orgasm in women involves a series of contractions in the uterus and vagina. A few women release a small amount of fluid from the vagina at the moment of orgasm.

30. **(c)** Men must go through a refractory period after orgasm; women can return immediately to orgasm if they choose. For both men and women, the resolution phase leads to a return to normal of pulse and breathing rates. The sex flush disappears; nipples, clitoris, and penis lose their erection; and the genitals revert to their normal color.

31. **(a)** *Sexual peak* is a term generally used to refer to the stage of life when a person is most easily aroused to orgasm. It is thought that this stage is later in women because orgasm in women is to some extent a learned response. (It doesn't seem fair, but there it is.) Although peaks vary among individuals, men most often peak between their late teens and their early 20s, whereas women peak anywhere from their mid-30s into their early 40s.

32. **(c)** According to various studies, approximately 70% of all women masturbate at least occasionally. They do this by stimulating the genital area in a variety of ways, from touching it with their fingers to pressing against a pillow to directing a spray of water onto the vulva and clitoris. Although some women insert something into their vaginas during masturbation, the great majority do not.

33. **(a)** As explained in the answer to question 30, women can move back to orgasm early in the resolution phase of sexual activity. If stimulation continues, a woman can proceed to have as many orgasms as she wishes.

The fact that all women are physically capable of this, however, does *not* imply that all or even most women have experienced it. An early Kinsey study held that between 8 and 9% of women reported having occasional multiple orgasms.

34. **(d)** Transsexuals do not get sexual arousal from wearing gender-inappropriate clothing, as do most transvestites; instead they feel that they are genuinely the opposite sex and simply have received the wrong organs. Sex change operations usually involve at least a year of hormone therapy before surgery. For a man who wishes to live as a woman, surgery removes the testicles and penis, using parts of the penis to build a clitoris and vagina. On a woman who wishes to live as a man, surgery changes the breasts; removes the uterus, Fallopian tubes, and ovaries; and may or may not involve constructing a (nonfunctional) penis. Transsexuals whose surgery is successful retain the nerve endings required for sexual stimulation and can achieve orgasm with their new bodies, although they are obviously infertile.

35. **(c)** Anal intercourse is fairly popular among heterosexual couples and gay men, although not as popular with either as is oral sex. Anal sex has some drawbacks, however — the rectum neither lubricates itself nor stretches as easily as the vagina, and thus the chance of small tears and other damage is more likely than with vaginal intercourse. This in turn leads to a possibility of infection and potentially easy transmission of AIDS or other STDs from an already infected partner. (The odds of this occurring are greatly reduced if a condom is worn. Also, in heterosexual intercourse, the man should wash between acts of anal and vaginal intercourse.) A woman cannot conceive *via* anal intercourse.

36. **(c)** The Latin term for "lust" is *libido*. *Coitus*, the word for the act of intercourse, means "a coming together." Most of our sexually-related terms derive from the Latin (a notable exception is *orgasm*, which has its roots in the Greek word for "to ripen.") Few words, however, have as negative an original meaning as *pudendum*, a word used to refer to the external genitals, especially the female genitals. A related English word is *pudency*, meaning "shame" or "modesty." In *Sex: The Facts, the Acts, & Your Feelings*, the author cites the original meaning of *testis*: "testament." Whereas a man's genitals were a testament to his manhood, a woman's were a source of shame.

37. **(b)** Sex drives vary among individuals, but a sex drive that interferes with daily life and cannot be satisfied even by repeated sexual acts to orgasm is called *hypersexuality*. The word refers to what was once called *nymphomania* in women and *satyriasis* in men.

38. **(b)** Erection difficulties can occur for many reasons, and it is only when all else has failed that penile implants may be recommended. One kind of implant, called semirigid, involves surgical implantation of silicone rods into the penis. With this implant, the penis is always erect. Another kind of implant is inflatable, activated with a pump mechanism. It should be noted that many men with erection difficulties have no trouble reaching orgasm, and mutually satisfying sex with a partner does not require an erect penis.

39. **(d)** Lack of sexual desire has been identified as a sexual problem separate from any physical manifestations thereof (impotence, etc.). The Kinsey Institute reports that, contrary to popular belief, just as many men as women have this problem. Therapeutic approaches vary depending on the underlying causes of inhibited desire. These causes may be physical and entail illness, depression, certain medications, or hormone imbalance. They may be emotional — anger, low self-esteem, boredom, and lack of trust may impede desire.

40. **(a)** Heterosexists — and they are in the majority in the United States — accept only heterosexual relationships as valid. Heterosexism wields a quiet hegemony over attitudes in this country by setting up expectations *via* the media and schools that all children will grcw up to marry and have children. Homophobes are people who are actually phobic or afraid of homosexuals. A number of studies have found that more than half of Americans, given a choice, would not allow homosexuals to teach school or enter the clergy. We will discuss prejudice and social attitudes at greater length in Tests 7 and 8.

In the Family Way: Pregnancy and Childbirth

wot in hell
have I done to deserve
all these kittens.

— *MEHITABEL THE CAT,*

as cited by Don Marquis

1. What is the role of the amniotic fluid in pregnancy?

   a. It protects the fetus.

   b. It produces hormones that regulate pregnancy.

   c. It transfers oxygen from mother to fetus.

   d. all of the above

2. What happens to the placenta after a normal vaginal delivery?

   a. It adheres to the uterus and is eventually absorbed.

   b. It shrinks to one-tenth its original size and is expelled over a period of days.

   c. It is delivered through the vagina just as the baby was.

   d. It is cut to pieces after the umbilical cord is cut.

3. When is a baby considered premature?

   a. when it is born before week 28 of pregnancy

   b. when it is born before week 37 of pregnancy

   c. when it has a birth weight under six pounds

   d. when it is born before the wedding

4. Amniocentesis may be used to diagnose

   a. Down's syndrome

   b. Tay-Sachs disease

   c. sickle cell anemia

   d. all of the above

5. Intercourse may be resumed after childbirth as soon as

    a. nursing has commenced

    b. healing is complete

    c. the baby is old enough to sleep through the night

    d. the menstrual cycle has resumed

6. More than three-fourths of all miscarriages occur

    a. from week 1 to week 12 of pregnancy

    b. between weeks 12 and 20 of pregnancy

    c. due to the mother's "incompetent cervix"

    d. after a fall or other injury to the mother

7. When might labor be induced?

    a. when a woman is in false labor

    b. when a baby is facing head downward

    c. when a baby is three weeks overdue

    d. all of the above

8. Why should pregnant women avoid alcohol and other drugs?

    a. These substances suppress the release of vital hormones.

    b. These substances can move across the placenta into the fetus.

    c. Women who abuse drugs go on to abuse their children.

    d. The risk of multiple births and late delivery increases dramatically in women who use drugs and alcohol.

9. Which diagram shows the breast of a pregnant woman?

a.

b.

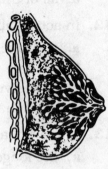

c.

d.

10. In the most common breech presentation,

   a. the fetus's head is nearest the cervix
   b. the fetus's feet are nearest the cervix
   c. the fetus's buttocks are nearest the cervix
   d. the fetus is facing the mother's back

11. In early labor,

   a. mild contractions begin
   b. the baby's head crowns

  c. the cervix dilates to 8 centimeters

  d. all of the above

12. In active labor,

  a. the urge to push begins

  b. the trip to the hospital may take place

  c. the cervix dilates fully

  d. all of the above

13. Transitional labor is

  a. the longest part of labor

  b. the shortest part of labor

  c. the stage at which delivery takes place

  d. when early labor fails to progress to active labor

14. What is quickening?

  a. the first time the mother feels the fetus move

  b. the increased flow of blood to the pelvis during labor

  c. a thin vaginal discharge common during pregnancy

  d. rapid weight gain during the second trimester

15. About what percentage of babies born in the United States are Caesarean births?

  a. between 1% and 2%

  b. between 5% and 10%

  c. between 10% and 20%

  d. over 30%

16. When a man and woman are unable to conceive, it is

  a. most likely due to the man's infertility

  b. most likely due to the woman's infertility

    c. most likely due to a basic physical incompatibility

    d. as likely to be caused by the man's infertility as by the woman's

17. Morning sickness generally affects

    a. nearly all pregnant women in the first trimester

    b. nearly all pregnant women in the third trimester

    c. about half of all pregnant women in the first trimester

    d. about one-tenth of all women throughout pregnancy

18. To what does the term in vitro fertilization refer?

    a. artificial insemination using the male partner's sperm

    b. artificial insemination using a donor's sperm

    c. fertilization outside of the body

    d. all of the above

19. In the United States, a woman may choose to have her baby delivered by

    a. an obstetrician

    b. a family physician

    c. a nurse-midwife

    d. any of the above

20. A patient in labor is about to have an epidural. What instruments will be used?

    a. a forceps and pliers

    b. a needle and plastic tubing

    c. a scalpel and a suction pump

    d. a plastic clamp and tweezers

21. What occurs in an ectopic pregnancy?

    a. The embryo grows outside the uterus.

    b. The embryo aborts spontaneously.

    c. Multiple eggs are fertilized.

    c. The fertilized egg blocks the cervical opening.

22. When a man experiences couvade, he

    a. is unable to father a child

    b. cannot make love to a pregnant woman

    c. is sexually stimulated by the thought of pregnancy

    d. mimics the symptoms of pregnancy

23. Approximately how often does a pregnancy result in twins?

    a. once in every 25 births

    b. once in every 90 births

    c. once in every 1,000 births

    d. whenever a woman has sex with two men on the same day

24. What happens when a pregnant woman is Rh-negative and the father is Rh-positive?

    a. The baby is born blind.

    b. The fetus can become anemic.

    c. The woman miscarries.

    d. The woman can become diabetic.

25. What is episiotomy?

    a. a surgical cut that enlarges the vaginal opening

    b. a form of anesthesia used in Caesarean births

    c. a drug used to induce labor

    d. a type of fetal monitor

26. What are the main hormones involved in pregnancy?

   a. testosterone and estrogen

   b. FSH, epinephrine, and thyroxine

   c. cortisone, glucagon, and vasopressin

   d. HCG, progesterone, and estrogen

27. How is the length of pregnancy determined?

   a. Count nine months from the last day of the last menstrual period.

   b. Count 42 weeks from the moment of conception.

   c. Count 40 weeks from the first day of the last menstrual period.

   d. Count back 40 weeks from the first day of the last menstrual period, add one year, subtract a week, and add twelve days.

28. How much weight should a woman gain during pregnancy?

   a. 5 to 15 pounds

   b. 15 to 20 pounds

   c. 20 to 30 pounds

   d. 35 to 45 pounds

29. What is the reason for chorionic villus sampling (CVS)?

   a. to check for maternal diabetes

   b. to check fetal heart rate

   c. to screen for birth defects

   d. to diagnose multiple fetuses

30. Which of these changes has taken place in the fetus by the end of the first trimester of pregnancy?

    a. The heart has begun to beat.

    b. Cartilage has turned to bone.

    c. Fat has built up in the face.

    d. all of the above

31. Which of these changes has taken place in the fetus by the end of the second trimester of pregnancy?

    a. The eyes can distinguish light.

    b. The face is fully formed.

    c. The fingernails extend beyond the fingers.

    d. The skin becomes smooth.

32. What is the risk of Down's syndrome in fetuses of women aged 35 to 40?

    a. 1 in 50

    b. 1 in 1,000

    c. 1 in 150

    d. 1 in 10

33. What is the main feature of Lamaze childbirth?

    a. use of a midwife

    b. strengthening the pelvic floor muscles

    c. control of breathing

    d. humane treatment of newborns

34. What percentage of women who attempt artificial insemination eventually become pregnant?

    a. 10 to 20%

    b. 30 to 40%

    c. 50 to 60%

    d. 70 to 80%

35. What is preeclampsia toxemia?

   a. fluid retention and a rise in blood pressure

   b. gestational diabetes

   c. anemia during pregnancy

   d. separation of the placenta from the uterus

36. What are Braxton-Hicks contractions?

   a. the contractions of labor

   b. uterine contractions during a miscarriage

   c. intermittent uterine contractions during pregnancy

   d. contractions that expel the afterbirth

37. What is colostrum?

   a. a milklike substance secreted from the breast

   b. the whitish substance covering a baby at birth

   c. a hormone that regulates milk supply

   d. a drug used to induce labor

38. Why is it valuable to obtain a sonogram during pregnancy?

   a. to confirm that a woman is pregnant

   b. to check the position of the fetus

   c. to check for birth defects

   d. all of the above

39. What is the function of the umbilical cord?

   a. to carry oxygen to the fetus

   b. to carry out the fetus's wastes

   c. to conduct nutrients from the mother to the fetus

   d. all of the above

40. What does a 10 on the Apgar scale indicate?

    a. a quickly-proceeding labor
    b. fetal distress
    c. good newborn health
    d. an inability to nurse

TEST 4: *Explanatory Answers*

1. **(a)** Shortly after fertilization, a sac grows around the developing zygote (the cell formed by the union of egg and sperm). The sac fills with a mixture of water, albumin (the same protein found in all egg whites), urea and creatinine (digestive byproducts), and some salts. Through the embryonic and fetal stages up until just before birth, the baby-to-be floats in this fluid, receiving the oxygen and food it needs *via* the umbilical cord. In 10 to 15% of pregnancies, the sac bursts before labor begins, releasing up to a quart of fluid through the vagina.

2. **(c)** The placenta is an organ for oxygen and nutrition exchange between mother and fetus. It is attached to the wall of the uterus and to the umbilical cord, which is attached to the fetus. Nutrition and oxygen pass through the placenta from mother to fetus; waste products pass through the placenta from the fetus to the mother. In a vaginal birth the placenta is delivered after the baby; contractions move it to the vaginal canal, and after the umbilical cord is cut and tied, the cord is often used to pull the placenta the rest of the way out. A placenta that attaches too far down in the uterus can cause bleeding and necessitate a Caesarean delivery. Such a condition is called *placenta previa*.

3. **(b)** Prematurity used to be defined by birth weight, with babies under 5½ pounds considered premature, but nutritional advances mean that today a baby born at 28 weeks might weigh 6 pounds or more. Usually, any baby born before week 37 is considered premature, but that does not presuppose that there will be some problem with the baby. The risk for very premature infants is due to the fact that their vital organs, particularly their lungs, have not matured completely. Today, however, it is not uncommon for very premature infants weighing less than 4 pounds to survive and thrive following neonatal care in the hospital. Factors associated with premature labor, as listed in *What to Expect*

When You're Expecting, include smoking, drug abuse, poor nutrition, inadequate weight gain, hormonal imbalance, infections, placenta previa, illness, stress, and prior premature delivery. Statistics cited in *Encyclopedia Britannica* indicate that in the United States, 7 to 9% of babies born to white mothers are premature, compared to 17% of babies born to black mothers.

4. **(d)** As it floats in the amniotic fluid, the fetus sheds cells, which can be extracted with a long hollow needle inserted into the mother's abdomen and through the uterine wall and placenta. The cells are then grown to allow a diagnostician to check for certain genetic abnormalities. Amniocentesis is usually performed between week 16 and week 18 of pregnancy on women who are over 35 or when mother or father has some history of genetically-carried disorders. Down's syndrome is caused by an aberration in the 21st chromosome. It is marked by mental deficiency and certain physical abnormalities. Down's syndrome has historically been more common in children born to women over 35, which is why the test is most often given to older pregnant women. (Some recent studies suggest that maternal age and the syndrome may not be as clearly connected as was once believed.) Tay-Sach's disease and sickle-cell anemia are both recessive traits, which means that if both parents are carriers, a baby has a 1-in-4 chance of having the disease. Amniocentesis can also be used to gauge fetal maturity if early delivery is recommended; it can disclose the sex of the fetus; and it can identify the presence of nearly one hundred additional congenital disorders. The procedure carries with it a slight risk of infection, which may lead to miscarriage.

5. **(b)** The vagina and cervix undergo a great deal of stress during vaginal delivery; small tears need time to heal before intercourse will be comfortable or risk-free. An episiotomy can mean additional pain during the first

few weeks after delivery. Usually doctors suggest a wait of at least three weeks before intercourse is attempted; many urge women to wait six weeks or more, to ensure that all cuts have healed and discharge (lochia) has ceased. A woman who is nursing may find that her vagina is drier than usual; a lubricant such as K-Y jelly may make intercourse more comfortable.

6. **(a)** Miscarriage, or spontaneous abortion, is far more common than you might imagine — perhaps one-third of all pregnancies end in miscarriage. Nearly all miscarriages occur during the first trimester. A woman may miscarry before she even realizes she is pregnant, but more often, miscarriage is traumatic for both parents. Reasons for miscarriage are many and varied. The fetus may be defective or damaged, or it may not have implanted properly in the uterus. The mother may be ill or have a hormonal imbalance. Factors such as smoking and poor nutrition are also thought to contribute to the risk of miscarriage. Late miscarriage — between weeks 12 and 20 — is usually due to problems with the placenta or the cervix. After week 20, what was called a miscarriage is considered a premature birth. Signs of miscarriage include heavy bleeding and pain in the lower abdomen. If the miscarriage is incomplete, a dilation and curettage (D and C) procedure may be required to remove any remaining tissue.

7. **(c)** Labor can be induced with infusion of the hormone oxytocin. This is done when a baby is sufficiently overdue that the placenta is too old and no longer transferring oxygen and nutrients to the baby; when the amniotic sac membranes have ruptured prematurely, which might lead to infection; when labor has gone on for a long time and then stopped; or when the health of the mother or the baby requires delivery before natural labor, such as when the mother is diabetic, Rh-negative with an Rh-positive baby, or showing signs of eclampsia (high blood pressure caused by pregnancy).

8. **(b)** The placenta is the link between mother and fetus, and it does not discriminate between things that are good for the fetus (oxygen and nutrients) and things that are bad for it (alcohol, cocaine, caffeine, and so on). Studies begun at the University of Washington in the early 1970s proved that alcohol can produce fetal alcohol syndrome, whose symptoms include mental retardation and physical defects. As many doctors and researchers noted in the 1980s, cocaine can kill a fetus, and a newborn with cocaine still in its system goes through withdrawal, which can kill it. Caffeine is a pretty powerful stimulant for an adult; a fetus, with its tiny size and its brain still in the process of development, is affected even more strongly. As early as 1973, Mount Sinai doctors cautioned women not to take any non-essential drug unless they were sure they were not pregnant. Different doctors give differing advice on the subject of occasional recreational drinking or caffeine use, but research proves that the potential danger to the fetus is extremely grave.

9. **(c)** During pregnancy, undifferentiated cells in the breast take on new roles in preparation for motherhood. Some become milk glands, some become milk ducts, and some become the sacs beneath the areola from which the baby will draw milk. The breasts swell, sometimes growing two or three cup sizes, and may sag slightly. For the first three or four days after delivery, a high-protein substance called colostrum is secreted by the breasts. Four to seven days after delivery, the breasts engorge as milk is first produced and breast tissue swells. If a mother decides not to breast-feed, her body will eventually reabsorb the milk and her breasts will gradually return to normal (as in Figure b). Figure a shows the undeveloped breast of a preteen. Figure d shows a breast after menopause.

10. **(c)** A fetus somersaults freely in the amniotic sac throughout pregnancy, but somehow 24 out of 25 babies

end up head first (called the vertex position) at the time of delivery. Occasionally a fetus presents with its buttocks down and its feet tucked up or straight up near its head. This breech position may mean that the head will not have time to compress slowly during the trip down the birth canal and may get caught on the pelvic bone. There is also a risk of the umbilical cord becoming tangled in the baby's arms and legs. Rarely, a breech baby will present one or both feet first. Many breech babies are delivered by Caesarean, but a small breech baby with no signs of fetal distress may be delivered successfully vaginally.

11. **(a)** Most women know that they are in labor when they feel irregular mild contractions. This phase of labor typically lasts from two to six hours, although women have been known to spend an entire day in early labor. During this time, the cervix dilates from 0 to 4 centimeters. (NOTE: The first phase of labor should not be confused with Braxton-Hicks contractions, weak, slow contractions that occur in the last few months of pregnancy and become more frequent as the pregnancy progresses. Some researchers believe that the contractions are the uterus's way of preparing for labor.)

12. **(b)** Most physicians and midwives encourage women to stay at home until their contractions are less than five minutes apart. During active labor, the cervix dilates from 4 to 7 centimeters, and contractions become stronger, lasting over a minute every three or four minutes. Active labor generally lasts three or four hours.

13. **(b)** Transitional labor is the part everyone warns you about, but luckily, it is usually over in under two hours. Strong contractions occur every two or three minutes, and it may feel as though there is no break between them. The cervix completes its dilation, expanding to 10 centimeters.

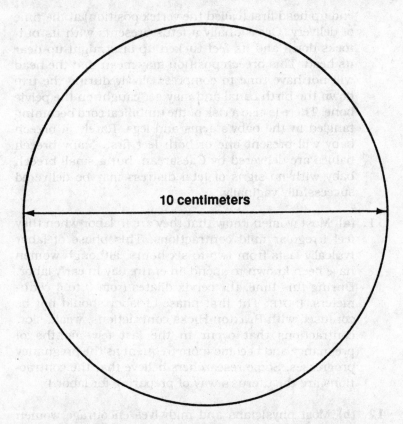

10 centimeters

At 10 centimeters, the urge to push kicks in, and the second stage of childbirth, pushing and delivery, takes place. Pushing and delivery may take up to two hours. The third stage of childbirth is the expulsion of the placenta.

14. **(a)** Fetal movements usually are felt first by the mother around week 20 of a pregnancy, although they may be felt earlier. A woman is usually aware of fetal movements after week 28 and should report to her doctor or midwife if they are not felt for one day after they have begun.

15. **(c)** Perhaps 10% of Caesarean deliveries, or C-sections, are needed because of fetal distress. The rest are due to a variety of complications: the mother's pelvis is too small to accomodate the baby's head; the mother has herpes; the baby is in breech position; and so on. A C-section is major surgery, but usually regional/spinal anesthetic is used and the mother can be awake throughout the procedure. A small incision is made low on the abdomen, the baby and the placenta are removed from the uterus, and the incision is stitched up. The whole procedure takes about an hour.

16. **(d)** *The Kinsey Institute New Report on Sex* reports that in about 40% of infertility cases, the problem is with the man, and in another 40% the problem is with the woman. About 10% of cases have no known cause, and in 10% of cases, both partners have a problem. If a couple has not conceived after a year of unprotected intercourse, they are advised to seek an evaluation. A general gynecologist or a family doctor can usually do the initial infertility evaluation and refer the couple to a fertility expert if necessary. In this country, about 20% of couples who try to conceive have difficulty doing so.

17. **(c)** Many people think that morning sickness is an inevitable part of pregnancy, but in fact, only about half of all pregnant women experience any degree of nausea during their terms. When it happens, morning sickness is usually worst during the first trimester (and not necessarily just in the morning, either!), and it may disappear entirely around week 12. Causes of morning sickness are unclear, but pregnancy hormones seem to increase acid production and slow down digestive activity. Doctors often recommend eating small, high-protein or high-carbohydrate meals several times a day to combat nausea.

18. **(c)** In 1977, Louise Brown was the first baby born *via* in vitro fertilization. In this process, an egg is taken from the ovary and fertilized with sperm in a Petri dish. The resulting embryo is then implanted in a woman's

uterus. The process is therefore meant for women whose Fallopian tubes are blocked but whose ovaries and uterus still function. Recently, however, a grandmother carried her daughter's baby to term, and surrogacy of this kind is likely to increase, along with its accompanying litigation. See Test 7 for more on surrogacy.

19. (d) A pregnant woman has a plethora of choices about where to have her baby. She can deliver at home with the care of a certified nurse-midwife or family physician; she can deliver at a free-standing birth center with a physician, obstetrician, or midwife; or she can deliver at the hospital. Obstetricians specialize in childbirth, but family physicians have training in obstetrics as well as general medicine. Many hospitals offer alternative birth centers — small, intimate, bedroom-like "birthing rooms." A woman may choose to give birth there rather than in a more clinical delivery or operating room. Complications in pregnancy or labor may require a change of plans regarding the birthing site.

20. (b) If anesthesia is needed because of severe pain in labor, it may be given in one of several ways. General anesthesia is given rarely, usually only for emergency Caesareans, because it relaxes the uterus and eliminates the contractions that move the baby down the birth canal. Regional anesthesia, injected into the spinal column, is more commonly used. Spinals, saddle blocks, or subdurals are all injections into the dura, the fibrous membrane that covers the spinal cord. Caudals or epidurals are injected into the space between the dura and the muscles that surround it. With some kinds of anesthesia, continuous drips may be used throughout part or most of labor. In such cases, the needle is inserted and then replaced with plastic tubing.

21. (a) In an ectopic pregnancy, the fertilized egg grows outside the uterus, usually in the Fallopian tube or ovary, but occasionally in the abdominal cavity. The condition can be caused by scarring of the Fallopian tubes from infection or endometriosis. The egg must be removed by surgery; if left untreated, rupture and internal bleeding will threaten the woman's life. The rate of ectopic pregnancy is rising, perhaps due to a rise in diseases that scar the reproductive organs; 1% of pregnancies are ectopic.

22. (d) Between 11% and 65% (in different studies) of expectant fathers experience couvade, from the French for "to hatch." In this syndrome, men mimic any or all of their pregnant partner's symptoms — nausea, vomiting, weight gain, food cravings, mood changes, and so on. The reason for couvade is not known, but theories include sympathy for or jealousy of the partner, anxiety, or stress.

23. (b) One-third of twins born are identical, formed from one fertilized egg and possessing identical genetic material. The other two-thirds are fraternal, born from two eggs. Fraternal twins have separate genetic makeups and can be of different sexes. The incidence of triplets in the population is one birth out of about 16,500; quadruplets occur once in every 718,000 births.

24. (b) Rhesus factor is a protein attached to red blood cells. (The name comes from rhesus monkeys, in whose blood the rhesus factor was first found.) If a woman is Rh-negative, lacking the substance, and her partner is Rh-positive, and one of their children born of a prior pregnancy is Rh-positive, the mother may produce antibodies to the Rh factor if fetal blood crosses the placenta. Then, if the next child is Rh-positive, the antibodies cross the placenta and attack the fetus's blood cells, making the fetus anemic. There is now a vaccine that can be given at 28 weeks of pregnancy and after the birth of the first Rh-positive child to prevent the formation of antibodies. For those Rh-negative women who did not receive the vaccine, their Rh-positive second child might need a blood transfusion. In emergency cases, this transfusion can be given *in utero*. Rh-negative women are also advised to have this vaccine after an abortion or miscarriage.

25. **(a)** In 1986, the rate of episiotomies in hospital births was 61%, but in midwife-assisted births, the figure was below 10%. Episiotomies are the subject of some controversy; they can cause pain, infection, scarring, and numbness. Studies show that only occasionally does an episiotomy positively affect the outcome of labor; for instance, when forceps are required or when the baby descends very quickly. In the past it was thought that a scissors cut in the perinium (the area between the vagina and the anus) was easier to repair than a tear, but most tears are now found to be straight and relatively easy to repair. An alternative to episiotomy is relaxation and massage of the perineum, and use of delivery positions other than the lithotomy (woman on her back on a table with her feet in stirrups), which places a great deal of pressure on the pelvic floor.

26. **(d)** At the moment of conception, the fertilized ovum releases HCG (human chorionic gonadotrophin), a pregnancy hormone that stimulates the release of progesterone, which helps to strengthen the uterine supports and allows it to expand. Estrogen also increases, helping the fetus, placenta, and mother's breasts to grow. After several weeks, the placenta produces its own progesterone and estrogen. Prolactin is produced by the pituitary gland and with oxytocin starts the supply of milk, and human placental lactogen, produced by the placenta, changes the mother's metabolism so the fetus receives enough nourishment.

27. **(c)** The medical description of the length of pregnancy is 280 days, or 40 weeks from the first day of the last menstrual period. This method of counting begins two weeks before conception probably occurs; that is, at the time of ovulation, which may confuse some women. The determination of due date is only approximate; a delivery is not considered late until the forty-second week is passed. The actual gestation period for the fetus is 38 weeks of growth.

28. **(c)** It is now thought that the safest amount of weight for a normal-weight woman to gain during pregnancy is 20 to 30 pounds, with 6 to 8 pounds being the fetus's weight and 14 to 24 being the weight of fluids, placenta and other products of pregnancy, and breast increase. A woman should gain approximately 3 to 4 pounds in the first trimester, 12 to 14 in the second, and 8 to 10 in the third. Overweight or underweight women or those with medical problems should have their weight gain carefully monitored.

29. **(c)** CVS is usually done in the eighth to twelfth week of pregnancy, though it can be done as early as the fifth week. Using ultrasound, a tube is inserted into the vagina to the uterus. A piece of the chorionic villi — the projections on the fetal membrane or chorion — is suctioned off and studied to determine if particular genetic birth defects are likely to occur. The miscarriage rate for this procedure is slightly higher than for amniocentesis — a difference of 0.8%.

30. **(a)** By the twelfth week of pregnancy, the fetus is between two and three inches long. Some of its vital organs are developed, though not fully; its eyes are widely placed in its face; its tooth buds are in place; and it can suck.

31. **(b)** By the end of the twenty-fourth week of pregnancy, the fetus's growth has slowed; it is about 13 inches long. It moves about energetically. Its body parts are in proportion, though it lacks fat, so its eyes seem prominent. In four weeks it will be considered legally viable.

32. **(c)** From puberty to age 25, the incidence of Down's syndrome, caused by an extra twenty-first chromosome, is 1 in 1,600. At 25 to 35 the incidence increases to 1 in 600; at age 35 to 40 it is 1 in 150; at 40 to 45 it is 1 in 100; and after age 45 it is 1 in 45. Amniocentesis is recommended for pregnant women over age 35 because at that age the possibility of the syndrome being present exceeds the possibility of miscarriage from the test.

33. (c) The Lamaze method of childbirth is a structured approach that focuses on control of the process, thus lessening fear of pain. Parents are educated about the birth process and taught to focus on breathing patterns. This intense concentration distracts the woman in labor from perceiving her pain and allows for oxygen supply to laboring muscles, preventing cramping. The other methods mentioned are the Bradley method, the Noble approach, and the Leboyer method.

34. (d) Although fewer than 20% of women trying artificial insemination conceive on the first try, the overall success rate for a healthy birth equals that in the general population. Use of frozen sperm lowers the success rate slightly but allows for more rigorous screening of the donor for disease and genetic history. Over 20,000 babies are born in the United States each year using donor insemination.

35. (a) Preeclampsia toxemia is a potentially dangerous condition in which a pregnant woman's blood pressure becomes elevated and she retains fluid. Its cause is unknown, though some researchers posit that it is connected with thinning of blood vessels in the placenta. It usually begins between the sixth and eighteenth week of pregnancy, and if untreated can block placental arteries, causing premature labor. The condition can progress to eclampsia, in which the mother has convulsions and can even lapse into a coma. Treatment of preeclampsia includes bed rest and careful monitoring.

36. (c) Braxton-Hicks contractions, often called "false labor," can occur any time after the second month of pregnancy but are usually most noticeable in the last trimester. They are often painless and work to aid circulation in the placenta and prepare the uterus for labor. As the birth approaches, they can segue into true labor.

37. **(a)** Colostrum is the substance secreted from the breast of a woman before her milk supply comes in. It contains antibodies and protein, and helps protect a newborn against some diseases. It also aids the baby's digestive system in emptying itself of mucus and meconium, a substance in the baby's bowels before birth. Occasionally a woman will secrete colostrum well before she gives birth.

38. **(d)** An ultrasound scan, or sonogram, works by bouncing sound off an object — in a pregnant woman, off the fetus. It can be used to view the fetus and estimate the delivery date based on its size. Certain defects, such as heart, spinal, and kidney abnormalities, can be seen on a sonogram. It can locate the position of the placenta if there is bleeding in the pregnancy and can determine if the fetus is in the breech position. Most practitioners believe ultrasound is safe for fetuses, but its long-term effects are still being studied.

39. **(d)** The umbilical cord, developed from the fetal cells, circulates blood, dissolved food, and oxygen to the fetus and carries off fetal wastes. The cord, therefore, allows the fetus to "breathe." Occasionally, a problem in delivery will develop when the cord is prolapsed — wedged between the cervix and the fetus. This cuts off blood supply to the fetus and often results in the need for a Caesarean delivery. Many doctors now recommend waiting to cut the cord until after birth, as this prevents a sudden cessation of oxygen to the newborn, but other doctors feel that waiting increases the possibility of jaundice in the baby.

40. **(c)** The Apgar scale, named after obstetrician Virginia Apgar, measures newborn heart rate, breathing, skin color, muscle tone, and reflexes, with 2 being the optimum score for each. The test is given at one minute and five minutes after birth. The maximum score is 10/

10; and a newborn with a score of 7/10 is in good health, 4/6 indicates a moderately depressed condition, and a score of 3 or below indicates a possibility of defects or later neurological problems.

Stop! In the Name of Love: Contraception

Contraceptives should be used on all conceivable occasions.

— *SPIKE MILLIGAN*

1. What is the average rate of pregnancy per 100 women over one year using spermicidal foams, jellies, and creams?
   a. 4%
   b. 11%
   c. 18%
   d. 25%

2. How does the contraceptive sponge work?
   a. It acts as a barrier against sperm.
   b. It absorbs semen.
   c. It kills sperm with spermicide.
   d. all of the above

3. What is the main advantage of Vaginal Contraceptive Film?
   a. It provides color photographs.
   b. It dissolves completely in the vagina.
   c. It contains a new, more effective spermicide.
   d. all of the above

4. What method is usually used in an abortion done in the first eight weeks of pregnancy?
   a. dilation and curettage
   b. dilation and evacuation
   c. vacuum aspiration
   d. saline injection

5. In most states, the legal difference between a menstrual extraction and an abortion is that a menstrual extraction
   a. does not require a positive pregnancy test
   b. is done before a period is missed
   c. is done by a nurse practitioner
   d. does not require notification of a spouse

6. How does NORPLANT work?

    a. A pill is taken once a month.

    b. A synthetic progesterone is implanted in a man's abdomen.

    c. A synthetic estrogen is injected into a man once a year.

    d. A synthetic progestin is implanted in a woman's arm.

7. What is the main ingredient in most spermicides?

    a. nonoxynol–9

    b. mestranol

    c. ethinyl estradiol

    d. norethindrone

8. Is there such a thing as a male birth control pill?

    a. No, there is no way to control sperm production.

    b. Yes, but most women do not trust men to use it.

    c. Yes, but its failure rate is over 20%.

    d. Yes, but it is only available in China.

9. When a man gets a vasectomy, what occurs?

    a. The seminal vesicles are emptied.

    b. The vas deferens is severed.

    c. The prostate is tied off.

    d. The sperm are treated to become infertile.

10. Which religious groups are urged to refrain from using birth control?

    a. Catholics

    b. Orthodox Jews

    c. some fundamentalist Christians

    d. all of the above

11. How many women, on average, using the condom as a contraceptive over a year, will conceive?

    a. all of them; the man must use the condom

    b. 25%

    c. 10%

    d. 5%

12. Can it be harmful to the fetus if a woman becomes pregnant while using contraception?

    a. no, unless the contraceptive is an IUD

    b. yes, unless the contraceptive is a condom used without spermicide

    c. no, unless the contraceptive is the birth control pill

    d. yes, no matter what contraceptive is used

13. How does RU486 work?

    a. It changes the makeup of the uterine lining.

    b. It blocks the passage of sperm through the cervix.

    c. It causes ovulation to cease.

    d. It opens the cervix, causing expulsion of the embryo.

14. What advantage does abstinence have as a method of birth control?

    a. It provides a chemical barrier against sperm.

    b. It has a failure rate of only 5%.

    c. It has a 100% effectiveness rate.

    d. There is no advantage.

15. Which of these actions can make a condom ineffective?

    a. using an oil-based lubricant

    b. using it for more than one act of intercourse

    c. not using it

    d. all of the above

16. What is the pregnancy rate per 100 women over the space of one year for the combined estrogen-progestin birth control pill?

    a. 2%

    b. 10%

    c. 12%

    d. 18%

17. Why isn't the contraceptive Depo-Provera approved for use in the United States?

    a. It has been proved to cause severe birth defects.

    b. It terminates rather than prevents pregnancy.

    c. It causes cancer in beagles.

    d. all of the above

18. What is the most widely used method of birth control?

    a. abstinence

    b. condoms

    c. *coitus interruptus*

    d. sterilization

19. Which of these are possible side effects of the birth control pill?

    a. abdominal rash and heavy menstrual flow

    b. fluid retention and gallbladder disease

   c. ringing in ears and low blood pressure

   d. painful intercourse and a decrease in blood clotting factors

20. How does the Minipill differ from the combination birth control pill?

   a. It contains only estrogen.

   b. It is only used as a morning-after pill.

   c. It has no side effects.

   d. It contains only progestin.

21. What holds a cervical cap in place?

   a. suction

   b. the forefinger

   c. a string from the uterus

   d. adhesive

22. How does a tubal ligation prevent conception?

   a. No pregnancy hormones are secreted.

   b. Eggs are kept apart from sperm.

   c. Production of eggs ceases.

   d. Sperm cannot leave the testes.

23. What happens to cervical mucus as ovulation approaches?

   a. It thickens and becomes cloudy.

   b. It turns clear and stringy.

   c. It disappears.

   d. It develops a cheesy consistency and odor.

24. Why might a thermometer play a role in contraception?

   a. When she is fertile, a woman's temperature rises.

   b. More sperm are produced in hot weather.

    c. Some women run a slight fever before menstruating.

    d. all of the above

25. Which of the following is an advantage of using an IUD?

    a. It prevents transmission of STDs.

    b. It can be left in place for a year or more.

    c. It can easily be inserted by a woman at home.

    d. all of the above

26. For a diaphragm to be effective if intercourse with ejaculation takes place more than once during a six-hour period,

    a. it must be removed and refilled with cream or jelly

    b. it must be removed, cleaned, and replaced

    c. it must completely fill the uterus

    d. contraceptive cream or jelly must be inserted into the vagina

27. Which method is usually used for very late abortions?

    a. vacuum aspiration

    b. dilation and curettage

    c. hysterotomy

    d. injection of saline or prostaglandin

28. If you use a rhythm method of contraception, what is the best way to avoid pregnancy?

    a. Abstain from intercourse before and during ovulation.

    b. Abstain from intercourse during and after ovulation.

    c. Abstain from intercourse during ovulation and menstruation.

    d. Abstain from intercourse for two weeks after ovulation.

29. What is a female condom?
    a. a condom packaged to appeal to women
    b. a condom contoured to provide pleasure to women
    c. a rubber vaginal liner
    d. a kind of dildo

30. Which method has been used to thwart pregnancy *after* unprotected intercourse?
    a. insertion of an IUD
    b. massive doses of DES
    c. menstrual extraction
    d. all of the above

31. Why should women not take sleeping pills while on the Pill?
    a. The interaction can cause nervousness and palpitations.
    b. Barbiturates interfere with the Pill's effectiveness.
    c. Because of the low level of barbiturate already in the Pill, the combination can lead to overdose.
    d. They could accidentally sleep through their entire cycle.

32. About one-third of all pregnancies in women who have been fitted with an IUD occur because

   a. the IUD has accidentally been expelled

   b. uterine changes have not had time to occur

   c. the IUD has been inserted backward

   d. the IUD string has been removed

33. What are a woman's chances of conceiving if she uses a diaphragm and spermicide correctly with every act of intercourse over the course of one year?

   a. 1 out of 1,000

   b. 1 out of 100

   c. 1 out of 50

   d. 1 out of 20

34. If a woman forgets to take the Pill on Friday, she should

   a. take a pill on Saturday and omit one pill at the end of the cycle

   b. start knitting booties

   c. take two pills on Saturday

   d. stop taking pills until the next cycle begins

35. Which of the following is a disadvantage of using the IUD?

   a. chance of pelvic inflammatory disease

   b. abnormal bleeding

   c. risk of ectopic pregnancy

   d. all of the above

36. Which of these services is *not* provided by Planned Parenthood?

   a. counseling

   b. sex education

    c. sex therapy
    d. gynecological exams

37. Is there such a thing as a contraceptive vaccine?
    a. Yes, and it is used by women in over 80 countries.
    b. Yes, but it is illegal in the United States.
    c. No, but vaccines for both men and women are being studied.
    d. No, but there are contraceptive injections for men.

38. Which of these statements about birth control is true?
    a. Taking the Pill after intercourse will prevent implantation.
    b. Certain medicated douches can kill sperm and prevent conception.
    c. Plastic wrap, if properly affixed, can be as effective a barrier as a condom.
    d. Some spermicides provide protection against diseases.

39. A vasectomy or a tubal ligation may be reversed by
    a. replacing the tubes with thin plastic tubing
    b. recutting, repairing, and reconnecting the tubes
    c. blowing gas through a needle into the blocked tubes
    d. none of the above

40. What do neo-Malthusians think about birth control?

   a. It is vital for the future of the planet.
   b. It runs against the teachings of the Talmud.
   c. It should be outlawed unless a woman's life is in danger.
   d. It is a woman's right.

TEST 5: Explanatory Answers

1. **(c)** Although spermicidal creams, suppositories, foams, and jellies can have a failure rate of only 3% if used correctly, the average failure rate is about 18%. Foam is probably slightly more effective than other spermicides because it forms a protective block against the cervix, but it loses its spermicidal effect after about 30 minutes, and so must be inserted just before intercourse. Creams and jellies are effective for six to eight hours.

2. **(d)** The contraceptive sponge, introduced in 1983, is inserted in the vagina to rest against the cervix. It contains spermicide, necessary because the sponge can be easily dislodged during intercourse. The sponge can be left in for up to 24 hours, during which time sexual intercourse can be repeated. Its disadvantages include the possibility of toxic shock syndrome and its failure rate, which is 10 to 20 failures per 100 women over one year.

3. **(b)** VCF, a relatively new contraceptive, consists of a square, thin vaginal film coated with spermicide. It is inserted into the vagina up to two hours before intercourse and dissolves there. It is as effective as creams and jellies and is less messy.

4. **(c)** In a vacuum aspiration abortion, a woman is usually given a local anesthetic in the cervix and perhaps an intravenous pain-killing drug. The cervix is dilated, and a cannula, or small tube, is inserted through it. A vacuum aspirator is attached and gently sucks out the contents of the uterus. Cramping, often painful, follows the procedure, and risks include infection, retained tissue, or missed abortion, in which the contents are not fully removed and the pregnancy continues.

5. **(a)** If a woman is fewer than three weeks past a missed menstrual period, she may request a menstrual extraction without a pregnancy test in most states. The extraction is similar to a vacuum aspiration abortion, though it may be done using a syringe rather than a

vacuum machine. The advantage to this procedure for many women is that it allows a woman to maintain ignorance about whether or not she is pregnant. Some feminists advocate menstrual extraction as a monthly procedure, making menstruation less uncomfortable and protracted, but the long-term effects of regular extraction are not yet known.

6. **(d)** NORPLANT, manufactured in Scandinavia, consists of six tiny rods containing levonorgestrel, a synthetic progestin. These are implanted in a woman's arm and release a small dose of hormone every day for about five years (less time if the woman is over normal weight). The hormone prevents ovulation about 60% of the time, makes the cervical mucus thicker, discouraging sperm passage, and changes the makeup of the uterine lining. Pregnancy rates are only 0.2 to 1.3 per 100 women over one year, and side effects are minimal to date. The implant was approved for use in the United States at the end of 1990.

7. **(a)** Most spermicides contain nonoxynol-9 as well as an inert agent that holds the spermicide against the cervix. Nonoxynol-9 destroys the membrane of sperm cells, and has the added effect of destroying the membranes of some bacteria and parasites, helping to protect against sexually transmitted diseases. Some studies, however, have raised the possibility that nonoxynol-9 might cause birth defects in offspring of women who conceive while using the spermicide. The other compounds mentioned are synthetic estrogens and a synthetic progestin.

8. **(d)** Gossypol, an impurity that occurs in cottonseed oil, was found to be an effective male birth control device in China in the 1950s, after a village of sterile men were found to have ingested oil made from cotton seeds that were not heated when pressed. Chinese scientists have tested the compound in pill form, and claim a 99% effectiveness rate. Some side effects, including low potassium levels, have been cited, and 10 to 20% of

men remain infertile after stopping treatment. This method, as well as other methods of male birth control, are in experimental stages in the United States, and are not expected to be available in the near future.

9. **(b)** The vas deferens (see diagram, p. 44), which brings the sperm into the ejaculatory duct, is cut in a vasectomy. The incision required is tiny and the operation, using a local anesthetic, takes only minutes. After it is performed, couples should use contraception for up to fifteen ejaculations, or until a microscopic test of the ejaculate confirms that there are no sperm remaining. The volume of semen diminishes by only 10% after a vasectomy, so the difference is barely noticeable. Despite the relative ease of the procedure, far fewer vasectomies than tubal ligations (the "tying" of a woman's Fallopian tubes, another form of sterilization) are performed each year.

10. **(d)** Both because of Biblical references, and because the concept of family is very highly regarded in these groups, certain religious denominations forbid the use of birth control, with the exception of natural family planning. Orthodox Jews refer back to Psalms 127:3–5, which states, "Happy is the man who has his quiver full of [sons]" and to the injunction, "Be fruitful and multiply." Some Orthodox Jews, however, do allow contraception for nursing mothers or child-wives. Catholics have been forbidden to use contraception by papal edict, reinforced strongly by Pope Paul VI in the encyclical *Humanae Vitae* (1968): "Every marriage act must remain open to the transmission of life." Certain fundamentalist Protestant groups also forbid the use of contraception on the same Biblical grounds as Orthodox Jews. See Test 8 for more on sex and religion.

11. **(c)** The condom is a fairly reliable method of birth control, more so when used with a contraceptive cream or jelly. Some brands now come coated with spermicide. Latex rubber condoms have the added virtue of pre-

venting transmission of venereal diseases, but either latex or animal skin condoms lose their effectiveness and can deteriorate over time or if stored incorrectly (in a wallet, for example, where body heat can make the condom brittle or sticky). Condoms should be stored in a cool, dry, dark place.

12. **(b)** Though the dangers of becoming pregnant while using spermicide are still under investigation, some studies indicate that nonoxynol-9, the main ingredient of most spermicides, may cause birth defects. Pregnancy while an IUD is in place results in a very high rate of miscarriage, and becoming pregnant while on the birth control pill may increase the possibility of congenital heart defects in the fetus, though again, studies on the problem are incomplete.

13. **(a)** RU486 (mifepristone) is a drug developed by a French doctor, Étienne-Émile Baulieu. The drug, administered early in pregnancy (five weeks or less), blocks absorption of progesterone by the uterine lining, causing it to slough off as in a menstrual period. In the initial French test of RU486, 85 of 100 women who took the drug for a period of two to four days aborted. A recent report in the *New England Journal of Medicine* states that in a study in which prostaglandins were also administered on the fourth day of treatment, 96% of pregnancies were terminated, 1% persisted, 2.1% aborted incompletely and required suction abortion or dilation and curettage, and 0.9% required blood transfusion from blood loss. RU486 is not available in the United States, nor is it likely to be in the near future, because pressure from anti-abortion groups makes drug companies fearful of boycotts that would harm their business.

14. **(c)** Abstinence, or refraining from sexual intercourse, is of course 100% effective in preventing pregnancy and has no side effects, except for an occasional nocturnal emission or nocturnal orgasm. Since the start of the

AIDS epidemic, and with the rise of other sexually transmitted diseases, discussed in Test 6, abstinence has become somewhat more popular, as has "dry sex," sexual relations that do not bring mucous membranes in contact with one another. Dry sex, however, can cause pregnancy if both partners are unclothed and the male ejaculates near the female's vaginal opening.

15. **(d)** Condoms are very thin sheaths, and their latex skins can quickly deteriorate if they come into contact with an oil-based lubricant. Water-based lubricants are recommended, and some condoms come pre-lubricated. A reservoir should be left at the tip of a condom when it is put on so that semen will not be forced down the sides of the penis and out at the bottom of the sheath. And, of course, a condom should only be used once, as sperm may be deposited inside it even without ejaculation, and it is weakened by use.

16. **(a)** Birth control pills prevent pregnancy by reducing the gonadotropin-releasing hormone (GnRH), which prevents the ovum from ripening. The synthetic hormones also change the makeup of the uterine lining and cause the cervical mucus to thicken, repelling sperm. Although the Pill has many known side effects, discussed in question 19, it also has some beneficial effects: it is thought to protect against uterine and ovarian cancers by regulating expulsion of the endometrium and blocking ovulation; it can aid women with endometriosis and those with irregular or painful periods; it can expedite absorption of calcium and decrease anemia because periods are lighter; and it lowers the incidence of pelvic inflammatory disease and ovarian cysts.

17. **(c)** Although Depo-Provera, an injectable synthetic progesterone, is used to treat uterine cancer, the FDA found that beagles given 50 times the recommended dosage of the drug had a high incidence of breast tumors — though beagles as a breed are very susceptible to breast tumors. Similar to NORPLANT in chemical structure, Depo-Provera is injected once every three months and causes ovulation to stop and the endometrium to thin. It can cause infertility for up to one and one half years after the last injection and may cause weight gain, depression, and headaches. It is used in over 80 countries as a contraceptive, but political pressure has delayed its acceptance in the United States.

18. **(c)** Withdrawal, or *coitus interruptus*, is not a particularly effective method of birth control. Per 100 women over a year practicing withdrawal, nearly 25 will conceive. There are several reasons for this: before a man ejaculates, sperm can be present in the pre-ejaculatory fluid. Furthermore, many men are not able to control their ejaculations and fail to withdraw in time. Finally, if the male partner ejaculates near the vaginal opening, sperm can still make their way up to the ovum. The Masters and Johnson squeeze technique, discussed in Test 3, can aid ejaculatory control for those couples whose circumstances or religion demand this method of contraception.

19. **(b)** Although side effects of the Pill were lessened in 1975 when a low-estrogen Pill was introduced, minor to serious complications can still arise. These include migraines, depression, fluid retention, yeast infections, fatigue, weight gain, acne, liver tumors, jaundice, heart attack, stroke, blood clots, gallbladder disease, and high blood pressure, among others. Because of these potential problems, the Pill is not recommended for women over 40, those who smoke, and those with heart disease. Doctors who prescribe the Pill should take care to give patients the formulation with the lowest possible effective dosage of estrogen and educate users on the early warning signs of dangerous complications.

20. **(d)** The Minipill, a progestin-only Pill, carries with it fewer side effects than the combination Pill. However, since it does not always prevent ovulation (it works by changing the uterine lining and thickening the cervical mucus plug), almost half of users experience break-through bleeding in between their usual periods. If pregnancy occurs during use, the possibility of the egg attaching to the Fallopian tube (ectopic pregnancy) is much higher than normal. Progestins are also impli-cated in heart disease among Pill users. The Minipill's failure rate is about 0.5% higher than that of the combination Pill.

21. **(a)** If a cervical cap is properly fitted, it will cover the cervix like a watchman's cap and be held in place by suction. Spermicide must be used with a cervical cap; if used properly, the cap has a success rate similar to that of a diaphragm. Unfortunately, its small size makes it more difficult to insert and place correctly, and it is far more likely than the diaphragm to be knocked out of place during intercourse. These facts combine to lower its typical success rate dramatically. Following intercourse, the cap should be left in place a minimum of six hours. Long popular in Europe, the cap is not yet widely available in the United States (it was approved by the FDA for sale in 1988). While it is made in several different sizes, not all women can use the cap because of variations in cervical shape and size.

22. **(b)** A tubal ligation seals or cuts the Fallopian tubes, keeping the eggs from ever connecting with invading sperm. In a woman who has "had her tubes tied," the egg never makes it from the ovaries to the uterus, but is instead absorbed by the body. Abdominal tubal lig-ation is major surgery. An incision is made in the abdomen, and the Fallopian tubes are tied off and cut. Laparoscopic tubal ligation and mini-laparotomy are done through smaller incisions and are less debilitating for the patient after surgery. A small incision is made very low on the abdomen, and a laparoscope is used to illuminate the uterus and Fallopian tubes. In laparos-copic ligation, heat is used to cauterize the tubes; in a mini-laparotomy, bands may be used to seal off the tubes. Rarely, a woman may have vaginal tubal ligation, in which the incision is made internally, near the cervix, and the Fallopian tubes are pulled through the incision, cut, tied, and replaced.

23. **(b)** Testing the cervical mucus and charting its changes is part of one natural method of contraception. After menstruation, little mucus is produced. As estrogen levels increase, mucus production increases. Just before ovulation and for a few days thereafter, the mucus is clear and elastic. This is the primary time when intercourse should be avoided if pregnancy is not desired. Following ovulation, the mucus clouds up and becomes much thicker. (A cheesy odor and consistency may indicate infection.)

24. **(a)** True, more sperm *are* manufactured during warm weather, even when a man lives and works in an air-conditioned environment (which suggests that it's light and not heat that causes the change). However, if you think a difference between 300 million and 150 million sperm will keep you from conceiving, think again — it only takes one! There *is* a form of contraception in which a woman records her basal body temperature each morning. Progesterone released around ovulation causes a tiny rise in temperature. (Usually the temperature dips slightly before rising.) During this period of higher temperature, a woman is fertile, and intercourse should not take place. Of course, many couples who *do* want a child use exactly the same method to determine their most fertile times for intercourse.

25. **(b)** An intrauterine device is a plastic or metal object inserted through the cervical opening into the uterus. Similar devices have been used as contraception for centuries (see Test 8). Little is really understood about the way in which IUDs prevent conception; they seem to cause an inflammation in the uterus that changes the uterine environment and may produce white cells that attack sperm. They certainly seem to interfere with implantation of fertilized embryos, but it does not seem likely that they cause "monthly miscarriages," as was once thought. Insertion is complicated and requires a doctor, but once successfully in place, the IUD may not need replacing for a year or more, making it truly a "no-hands" means of contraception. It does *not*, however, prevent the spread of sexually transmitted diseases, including AIDS, and may even predispose a woman to PID if bacteria climb up the string into the uterus and the Fallopian tubes.

26. **(d)** A diaphragm is a round rubber dome that covers the cervical opening to the uterus, thus barring the door to eager sperm. It is always used with spermicidal cream or jelly, because sperm are able to swim around the edges no matter how tightly the diaphragm fits. A diaphragm can be put in place up to six hours before intercourse; if any more time elapses, the spermicide may be too depleted to be helpful. The diaphragm should be left in place for at least six hours after intercourse to ensure that no straggling sperm get by the barrier. If intercourse is repeated during that time, additional cream or jelly should be added with a syringe, but the diaphragm should *not* be moved or removed.

27. **(d)** If a pregnancy is terminated between week 16 and week 24, the usual procedure is to induce a miscarriage. A solution of saline, prostaglandin, or urea is injected into the amniotic sac. The injection causes the uterus to contract as in labor, expelling the fetus and placenta.

28. **(a)** Rhythm methods, whether based on temperature or on the calendar, have miserable success rates. Typically, one woman in four who use this form of contraception will become pregnant within a year. It is difficult to measure such small temperature changes accurately, and many people do not take into account the fact that sperm can live in a woman's body for days after the last act of intercourse. Because of this latter fact, the best way to avoid pregnancy is to avoid intercourse during

the time before and during ovulation, an option that makes only about two to two and one-half weeks out of each month "safe."

29. (c) "Femshield," a British-made, condom-shaped vaginal liner, is currently undergoing tests and may soon be available in the United States. Femshield looks like a condom with a rubber ring on each end, one of which is closed. The closed end is inserted with the help of the rubber ring and pushed into the vagina much as a diaphragm would be. The open end dangles just outside the vagina. Presumably, Femshield will have a success rate similar to that of "male" condoms.

30. (d) Diethylstilbestrol (DES), a form of synthetic estrogen, was the original morning-after pill. Its side effects, as with other such high-estrogen-dose therapies, include nausea, cancer risk, and potential harm to the fetus if a miscarriage does not take place and pregnancy continues. As with morning-after pills, insertion of an IUD is meant to keep the embryo from implanting in the uterus, but should it fail, the fetus may be endangered by the presence of the IUD. Menstrual extraction may be used if the period does not take place as scheduled. None of these methods is recommended, and morning-after pills are considered so dangerous that they are now rarely used except in cases of rape.

31. (b) Barbiturates and such commonly prescribed antibiotics as ampicillin and tetracycline can interfere with estrogen absorption and limit the Pill's effectiveness as a contraceptive. The same appears to be true of certain drugs prescribed for anxiety (such as Miltown) and epilepsy (such as Dilantin). The Pill appears to slow down metabolism and absorption of certain drugs such as Valium, Librium, alcohol, and caffeine, leading to overdose from what had been considered a normal dose of the drug.

32. (a) The IUD is often expelled from the body at the first or second menstruation after insertion, and if this is not noticed and intercourse takes place, pregnancy may ensue. If it remains correctly in place, the IUD has a success rate of 95 to 98%, better than the diaphragm and somewhat worse than the Pill.

33. **(c)** If a diaphragm is used absolutely correctly every single time, it is about 98% effective; that is, out of 100 women, 2 will become pregnant over a period of a year using this method. In reality, though, things go wrong; women forget to reinsert spermicide, the diaphragm does not fit properly or shifts during intercourse, a couple takes a chance and neglects to use the diaphragm at all. This brings the actual observed risk of pregnancy per act of intercourse to between 1 in 10 and 1 in 5.

34. **(c)** It's not recommended, but it is possible to play "catch-up" with the Pill as long as only one or two pills have been missed. If two pills have been missed, a woman can take two one day and two the next to catch up, but should probably also use spermicide or a barrier method of contraception for the rest of the cycle just to be sure.

35. **(d)** IUDs have a bad reputation, although the study that led to the reputation is now under attack. Once there were several types sold in the United States; now only two types are available. Deaths attributed to infection caused by the Dalkon Shield led to its being removed from the market, and subsequent lawsuits (see Test 7) prompted other manufacturers to get out of the IUD business. IUDs clearly lead to a higher risk of infection and pelvic inflammatory disease. Abnormal, heavy bleeding and pain are often reported by users. Sometimes a woman becomes pregnant with the IUD in place; usually this leads to miscarriage, but often the pregnancy is ectopic, with the embryo remaining in the Fallopian tube rather than descending into the hostile uterine environment.

36. **(c)** The Planned Parenthood Federation of America was formed in 1942 from a merger of Margaret Sanger's

clinics and the National Birth Control League (see Test 8). It operates about 700 clinics nationwide and is part of the International Planned Parenthood Federation. Clinics provide counseling, access to birth control, gynecological checkups and related medical diagnosis and prescription, and sex education programs. Planned Parenthood also sponsors an active lobbying group and supports research into new methods of birth control.

37. (c) Vaccines for men and women and shots for men are the focus of a good deal of birth-control research, funding for which has all but dried up in recent years. Shots for women already exist (see question 17) but are not legal in the United States despite their effective use in more than 80 countries worldwide.

38. (d) Nonoxynol and octoxynol, ingredients in some spermicides, appear to be effective in preventing transmission of some sexually transmitted diseases. Taking a single birth control pill is useless; the efficacy of the Pill depends on its being used in a complete cycle. Douching will not prevent conception and may even speed the sperm up the vagina to the uterus. As the new Kinsey Report points out, all plastic wrap contains tiny holes big enough for sperm to swim through, so plastic wrap is absolutely worthless as a barrier method.

39. (b) Reversal of sterilization is a difficult and costly procedure, and the results are not always satisfactory. Tubes are often scarred and damaged after sterilization, and to cut out the damaged part and reconnect the tubes requires major surgery by a qualified microsurgeon. Not all patients who ask for such a reversal can have it performed; whether it will work depends on the original method and location of the tube-tying as well as the condition of the tubes. The success rate in reversals of vasectomies is somewhat higher than for reversals of tubal ligations — the Kinsey Report states that perhaps 75% of vasectomy reversals result in eventual conception.

40. **(a)** In his 1798 *Essay on the Principles of Population,* Thomas Malthus said, "Population, when unchecked, increases in a geometrical ratio. Subsistence increases only in an arithmetical ratio." Malthusians believe that the earth's resources are finite and threatened by the burgeoning human population. Malthus himself was not a proponent of birth control; he advocated moral restraint (late marriage and abstinence), considering contraception and abortion "vice." Malthusian Leagues formed throughout Europe in the nineteenth century, leading to the establishment of family planning associations. Neo-Malthusians such as Paul Ehrlich in this century have kept the argument alive by projecting appalling population increases and their potential outcomes into the next millenium. Increased awareness and incentive programs have actually decreased the birth rate from over 2% in 1970 to 1.6% in 1985; however, the rate in Africa and Latin America is still over 2%. Rates have decreased most in countries where industrialization has accompanied education and family planning help: Trinidad, Jamaica, Puerto Rico, South Korea, Hong Kong, and Singapore have had successful programs. In 1948, Japan was the first country to establish a nationwide family planning policy. Japan continues to rely on abortion as a major means of birth control; most countries today with a nationwide policy rely on oral contraceptives. "Zero population growth" has been a goal in China for the past 20 years, aided by a stringent "one child per couple" regulation.

Let's Get Tested: Sexually Transmitted Diseases

Make War, Not Love — It's Safer.

— 1980s BUMPER STICKER

1. Why might certain sexually transmitted diseases be more dangerous for women than for men?
   a. Men are twice as likely to seek medical attention.
   b. Women may harbor STDs without knowing it.
   c. Women are more susceptible to massive infection.
   d. Men are better adapted to having multiple partners.

2. Which of the following is *not* usually an early symptom of HIV infection?
   a. diarrhea
   b. swollen glands
   c. night sweats
   d. genital sores

3. Hepatitis-B can be transmitted through anal intercourse or through
   a. injection with a used needle
   b. anal-oral sex
   c. transfusion of infected blood
   d. all of the above

4. Which of the following is *not* true of pubic lice?
   a. You can get them from a toilet seat.
   b. The cure does not require a prescription.
   c. They are often found on the head as well.
   d. They feed on blood.

5. A man infected with gonorrhea will usually
   a. run a high fever
   b. feel pain when urinating

    c. develop a sore on the penis or scrotum

    d. all of the above

6. Many states require a blood test for syphilis before granting a marriage license because

    a. a child born to a syphilitic mother may be deathly ill

    b. the Centers for Disease Control wish to monitor the disease

    c. this allows a couple to decide against marriage on the grounds of unfaithfulness

    d. syphilis can cause brain damage

7. At the end of the 1980s, about how many cases of gonorrhea were reported annually in the United States?

    a. 75,000

    b. 750,000

    c. 7.5 million

    d. 75 million

8. A woman who develops a rash on her inner thighs soon after sexual intercourse may be experiencing

    a. an allergic reaction to semen

    b. "honeymoon cystitis"

    c. the first signs of a syphilitic infection

    d. an outbreak of herpes

9. Pregnant women and recent brides are especially prone to contracting

    a. gonorrhea

    b. chlamydia

    c. urinary tract infections

    d. to have the house redone

10. Which of the following is true of herpes simplex II?

    a. It may be transmitted from genitals to mouth.

    b. It may be transmitted from genitals to genitals.

    c. It may be transmitted from mouth to genitals.

    d. all of the above

11. You are most at risk for sexually transmitted diseases if

    a. you are gay

    b. you are a teenager

    c. you have more than one sexual partner

    d. you have anal sex

12. If you are diagnosed as having NGU, you will probably be given

    a. a topical salve or ointment

    b. aspirin or another mild painkiller

    c. tetracycline or another antibiotic

    d. electroshock therapy

13. What do chancroid and syphilis have in common?

    a. They are bacterial infections.

    b. Both produce chancres on the genitals.

    c. They are among the most prevalent STDs.

    d. all of the above

14. Gardnerella is a type of

    a. fungus

    b. vaginal infection

    c. bacteria

    d. sexually transmitted virus

15. A woman's first sign of trichomoniasis is usually
   a. itching and a frothy discharge
   b. pain during intercourse
   c. small bumps on the labia
   d. inability to void the bladder

16. What do these drugs have in common: alpha interferon, dextran sulfate, ampligen?
   a. They are all antibiotics used to treat STDs.
   b. They are all being tested as possible AIDS therapies.
   c. They all cure AIDS-related pneumonias.
   d. They are all illegal in the United States.

17. What are scabies?
   a. small, itchy bumps left behind by crab lice
   b. parasitic mites
   c. encrustations over herpes lesions
   d. ulcerations of the gums, a sign of stage-2 syphilis

18. A primary symptom of LGV is
   a. pimple-like growths on the genitals
   b. a purple rash on the lower extremities
   c. blood in the urine
   d. a sudden drop in blood pressure

19. The suffix -*itis* in the name of a disease means
   a. inflammation
   b. injury
   c. passageway
   d. bacterial

20. If you are a heterosexual woman who does not use drugs,

    a. you are not at risk for AIDS

    b. you are less at risk for AIDS than if you were a lesbian

    c. you are ten times less likely to contract AIDS than a heterosexual man who does not use drugs

    d. you are more at risk for AIDS than a heterosexual man who does not use drugs

21. Which of the following is the most prevalent viral sexually transmitted disease in the United States?

    a. endometriosis

    b. mononucleosis

    c. genital warts

    d. syphilis

22. Why is cytomegalovirus especially dangerous in pregnant women?

    a. It can infect the fetus, causing birth defects.

    b. It can cause the mother to go into premature labor.

    c. It can block the birth canal, requiring a Caesarean birth.

    d. It can cause separation of the placenta from the uterine wall.

23. Which of the following is *not* true of yeast (candida) infections?

    a. They can occur as a result of taking oral antibiotics.

    b. The *Candida* organism is present in many healthy women.

    c. They cause itching and discharge.

    d. The infection is highly contagious.

24. By which of these pathways can AIDS *not* be transmitted?

    a. by massaging an infected person

    b. by sexual intercourse with an infected person

    c. by blood transfusion with infected blood

    d. by sharing a needle with an infected person

25. Which of these is the most common sexually transmitted disease in the United States?

    a. genital herpes

    b. gonorrhea

    c. chlamydia

    d. AIDS

26. What is the main symptom of molluscum contagiosum?

    a. painful urination

    b. thick vaginal discharge

    c. urge to eat shellfish

    d. raised itchy rash

27. What are the symptoms of genital herpes?

    a. odoriferous discharge and hair loss

    b. painful sores, burning urination, and muscle pains

    c. Herpes is usually asymptomatic.

    d. rash, sore throat, and rectal bleeding

28. After homosexual men, which of these populations has the highest incidence of AIDS?

    a. intravenous drug users

    b. hemophiliacs

    c. blood transfusion recipients

    d. heterosexuals

29. Which of the following can cause pelvic inflammatory disease (PID)?

    a. candida and herpes

    b. condyloma and chancroid

    c. gonorrhea and chlamydia

    d. all of the above

30. From which of these STDs will use of a condom during intercourse *not* give protection?

    a. crabs

    b. gonorrhea

    c. syphilis

    d. gardnerella

31. Which of these STDs can contribute to male infertility?

    a. genital herpes

    b. chlamydia

    c. candida

    d. condyloma

32. If you contract granuloma inguinale you are likely to suffer

    a. vaginal bleeding and discharge

    b. severe itching

    c. lymph node swelling and raised sores

    d. high fever and abdominal tenderness

33. Which of these activities does *not* put a lesbian at risk for contracting AIDS?

    a. becoming pregnant by donor insemination

    b. massaging and hugging a lover

    c. practicing cunnilingus on a lover

    d. sharing needles

34. Which of the following could be considered a practice of safer sex?

    a. mutual masturbation

    b. oral sex

    c. anal sex

    d. fisting

35. What symptoms identify the third stage of syphilis?

    a. a sore and enlarged lymph nodes

    b. a rash and gray patches on mucous membranes

    c. hair loss, fever, and fatigue

    d. nerve damage, blindness, and psychosis

36. Which of these STDs is linked to cancer?

    a. genital warts

    b. chlamydia

    c. gonorrhea

    d. all of the above

37. An infected mother can pass on to her fetus or newborn

    a. gonorrhea

    b. syphilis

    c. AIDS

    d. all of the above

38. Which of these sexual practices is most likely to result in an STD infection with an enteric pathogen such as shigellosis?

    a. cunnilingus

    b. oral-anal sex

   c. rear-entry intercourse

   d. masturbation

39. The symptoms of a mycoplasma STD

   a. include weight loss and heavy bleeding

   b. are similar to those of a yeast infection

   c. are similar to those of chlamydia

   d. are only evident in men

40. When does practicing oral sex put one at high risk for an STD?

   a. only when one partner has syphilis

   b. only when one partner has AIDS

   c. only when one partner has a viral STD

   d. when either partner is infected with any STD

Test 6: Explanatory Answers

1. **(b)** A majority of women with gonorrhea, pelvic inflammatory disease, and certain other STDs show no symptoms at all. Unless the disease is found through routine testing, these women risk permanent damage to their reproductive systems. Men tend to show symptoms of disease soon after infection, mainly because their genitals are more clearly visible, and lumps, sores, or discharges are more easily observed. However, some men, too, are asymptomatic, so simply examining the penis for signs of infection will *not* protect a sexual partner from potential disease.

2. **(d)** The human immunodeficiency virus (HIV) that causes AIDS is a very slow-acting virus that rests perhaps for years in certain immune-system cells before waking up, reproducing, and destroying its host cells and eventually its human host. Because of its slow action, the virus may not cause many symptoms in a newly-infected person, but some people have symptoms not unlike a mild case of the flu. These symptoms may fade and vanish for years. Then as the dormant virus wakes up and begins destroying immune cells, its host human begins to experience increasingly catastrophic infections, which may include shingles, serious gastric disorders, pneumonia, and tumors. A person who is HIV positive may infect sexual partners whether or not he or she shows any symptoms of disease.

3. **(d)** Like HIV, hepatitis-B is a potentially deadly virus that is found in human blood products. Its transmission from an infected partner to a healthy partner *via* anal sex makes it especially prevalent among gay men. The virus attacks the liver, causing jaundice, fever, muscle aches, and extreme fatigue. In its rare, fatal or *fulminant* form, hepatitis-B kills a victim within six weeks. Ten percent of all hepatitis-B-infected people become carriers of the disease, and of these, according to *Modern Prevention*, nearly 25% will eventually die of related

liver cancer or cirrhosis. The Centers for Disease Control report that despite the existence of an effective vaccine, the number of new cases of hepatitis-B each year hovers around 300,000. Use of a latex condom can prevent the transmission of hepatitis-B.

4. (c) Lice have very specific tastes, and pubic lice, commonly known as "crabs" because of their shape, prefer the pubic region. Crabs can be transmitted through sexual contact or contact with an object that has been used by an infested person — a toilet seat, a towel, and so on. The lice latch on to the roots of pubic hairs and begin to suck blood. Females lay eggs daily, which take about a week to hatch, so it does not take long before a host is truly infested. Lice are tiny but can be seen with the naked eye, and their bites may cause intense itching and a rash. Over-the-counter medicated lotions and shampoos quickly kill the lice and their eggs and alleviate the itching.

5. (b) The most common symptoms of gonorrhea in men are a milky discharge from the penis and pain during urination. Gonorrhea, commonly called "the clap" (from the Old French word *clapoir*, meaning "venereal sore"), is caused by the bacteria *Neisseria gonorrhoeae*. It generally manifests itself as a discharge that is highly contagious and can spread infection to the eyes as well as to areas involved in sexual activity. Many women show no symptoms, but those who do may have a thick discharge and redness around the cervix, or a sore throat and swollen glands if the infection was passed on during oral sex. Left untreated, gonorrhea may lead to pelvic inflammatory disease in women and thence to sterility by scarring the Fallopian tubes. Gonorrhea is treatable with various antibiotics, but new, robust strains have developed recently that are resistant to the drugs most often used in treatment.

6. (a) Although b, c, and d may well be true, the reason some states still require a blood test for syphilis has to do with the dangers of syphilis to infants. A baby infected during pregnancy may be stillborn, or it may be born with a variety of handicaps and disfigurements. Early testing allows for speedy treatment, and even treatment during pregnancy itself can lead to a healthy baby. These days, with so many infants born to unwed mothers, the marriage test is somewhat less useful. Many doctors require a test as soon as a woman becomes pregnant, whether she is married or not.

7. **(b)** According to the Centers for Disease Control, 734,014 cases of gonorrhea were reported in the United States in 1989. Keep in mind that not all cases are reported; the disease may go untreated in some people who show no symptoms and continue to pass it on to others. In 1981, the author of *Sex: The Facts, the Acts, and Your Feelings* reported that about 2 million Americans contracted gonorrhea each year. Whereas gonorrhea is in decline (except, as noted by the CDC, in urban minority populations, where it is still epidemic), reported cases of chlamydia, herpes, and genital warts have increased steadily over the last decade.

8. **(a)** People with a high incidence of other allergies are occasionally allergic to semen. As with any other allergy, the body is working to reject a foreign substance, manufacturing histamines that produce a rash or other allergic symptoms. It is far *more* common to develop an allergy to spermicides or to the latex in condoms and diaphragms. In such cases, alternative birth control methods must be tried. In the case of people with allergies to their partners' semen, the partner may wear a condom, or injections made from his semen may be concocted to desensitize his partner.

9. **(c)** Urinary tract infections, of which the most common is cystitis, are especially common in pregnant women because of the pressure of the fetus on their bladders and newlyweds because of their increased sexual activity. The symptoms include severe pain on urination, a constant urge to urinate, and (sometimes) blood or pus

in the urine. Generally, *Escherichia coli* bacteria are the culprits responsible; they live in the rectum and can travel up the urethra to the bladder and kidneys. Any unusual irritation of the urethra (as in sexual activity) or the bladder (if urine is not completely voided) will cause the bacteria to grow. Women prone to UTIs are advised to urinate before and after any sexual activity, and in some cases, to forego use of a diaphragm, which may press against the urethra or bladder. Various antibiotics may be used to treat the infections.

10. (d) Herpes simplex II is most commonly known as genital herpes, whereas herpes simplex I is the virus that causes cold sores and fever blisters, but *either* herpes virus may be transmitted between mouth and genitals during oral sex.

11. (c) Merely being young, or being gay, or engaging in anal intercourse is not enough to put a person in danger for STDs. The most dangerous behavior is that involving multiple partners, for the odds of STD infection increase as each new partner and his or her accompanying sexual history is introduced. Young people have more STDs than older people because they are less likely to have settled down with a single partner. Gay men with a single steady partner are rarely at risk for STDs. Anal intercourse is only dangerous if it involves penetration by or of an infected partner.

12. (c) Moving up fast on the list of most prevalent STDs is nongonococcal urethritis (NGU), a catchall term for any bacterial infection of the urethra *not* caused by *Neisseria gonorrhoeae*. The most common source of the infection is *Chlamydia trachomatis* (see question 25), but various other organisms may be responsible. Symptoms, *when they occur*, may be similar to those in cases of gonorrhea — pain during urination and some kind of discharge. NGUs generally respond to tetracycline or erythromycin, but lab tests are vital to make sure the medication is the correct *coup de grâce* for whichever infecting organism is found.

13. (d) This is another example of why it is important to have tests done and get an accurate diagnosis if you think you have an STD. Syphilis and chancroid are caused by different bacteria (*Treponema pallidum* and *Hemophilus ducreyi*, respectively) and not all antibiotics will kill both types of bacteria. Chancres are the highly infectious, pus-filled sores on the genitals or around the anus that are primary signs of both diseases. Chancroid (meaning "like chancres") may be painful but is not nearly as serious as syphilis. *The New Our Bodies, Ourselves* lists chancroid on its chart of most common STDs. If CDC studies are correct, this appears to be due to a rise in outbreaks of chancroid among urban and migrant poor.

14. (b) *Gardnerella vaginalis* used to be called *Hemophilus vaginalis* after the *Hemophilus* bacterium that is its cause. *Hemophilus* is a nasty genus; other species of *Hemophilus* are responsible for pinkeye, some meningitis, and chancroid. *Gardnerella* is closely related. The disease is generally marked by a gray-colored, foul-smelling discharge. As with many such diseases, reinfection is possible unless the sexual partner is treated with antibiotics along with the person exhibiting the symptoms.

15. (a) *Trichomonas vaginalis* is a protozoan that is usually transmitted sexually, often from an asymptomatic man to a woman who will soon exhibit itching; redness; and a strong-smelling, foamy, white, gray, or yellowish discharge. The usual treatment is metronidazole (trade name Flagyl), a very strong drug with many potential side effects, and one that may *not* be taken by pregnant women or women who are breastfeeding babies. One massive dose is usually enough to knock out the infection; sexual partners should also be treated to avoid reinfection.

16. (b) As the search for an AIDS vaccine goes on, probably into the next century, a variety of drugs with different mechanisms for attacking HIV are being tried out in small test groups across the country. One of the few that is in widespread use is the extremely toxic AZT, which seems to protect immune-system cells from destruction by HIV. While it is not a cure, AZT has apparently prolonged the lives of certain AIDS patients. Different groups of researchers are concentrating on different stages in the life of the HIV virus, hoping to discover one point at which the virus is most vulnerable to attack. Dextran sulfate appears to stop the virus from initially binding with the host cell. Alpha interferon may keep the virus from reproducing. Ampligen causes cells to produce their own interferon, which then inhibits reproduction of the virus. These and many other drugs are being tested; but many citizens argue that the testing process is too slow and too restricted — not enough people are allowed to test the drugs, not enough women and children are being tested, there is not enough money for research, and so on.

17. **(b)** Like lice, mites can be passed on through physical contact with an infested person or object. Because a primary infestation may not produce symptoms for weeks, many people may unknowingly be infested by a single carrier. The mites burrow under the skin and lay their eggs. Scabies first shows up as intensely itchy raised bumps on the skin. Treatment with topical ointments is usually effective within a few days.

18. **(a)** Lymphogranuloma venereum (LGV) is a disease in the family of Chlamydia that affects the mucous membranes and lymph glands. Usually a small growth on the skin accompanied by fever and flulike aches is the first sign of infection. LGV is often misdiagnosed as syphilis or chancroid and may therefore be hard to eliminate. Usually tetracycline, an antibiotic, is used in treatment.

19. **(a)** Inflammation is the swelling, redness, and pain that results from an injury or infection. The suffix *-itis* appears in many names of STDs; by understanding the roots of the name, you can understand the nature of the ailment. For example, *epididymitis* is an infection of the epididymis, *prostatitis* is an infection of the prostate, *urethritis* is an infection of the urethra, and *vaginitis* is an infection of the vagina. Unlike some disease names, such as gonorrhea or chlamydia, these names do not specify the cause of the disease; they merely indicate its location.

20. **(d)** As of October 31, 1990, fewer than one-tenth of reported AIDS cases were in women, and the majority of those were in women who used intravenous drugs. However, of the slightly over 8,000 reported cases of AIDS in heterosexuals, 4,810 were in women. All other things being equal, we know that heterosexual women are simply more likely than heterosexual men to become infected with *any* STD in a single act of intercourse with an infected partner; a woman with multiple partners is more at risk for STDs than a man with multiple partners. For more on AIDS populations, see questions 28 and 33.

21. **(c)** Human papilloma virus, also known as condyloma or genital warts, is an extremely infectious STD. It is quickly becoming one of the most common STDs in America; almost 3 million people a year are infected with it. Often, HPV is asymptomatic, as the warts can be very small, even invisible to the naked eye, and can be confined to the inner vagina or cervix. Sometimes the warts itch or burn, and they can grow very large. During pregnancy growth can be stimulated by hormones; very rarely they can cover the vulva and block the vaginal opening, making vaginal delivery impossible. In men, they commonly appear on the glans, foreskin, and urethral opening. Treatments for HPV include topical liquids, cryosurgery (freezing), heat cauterization, and laser surgery. Warts often recur after treatment, but occasionally they will spontaneously regress.

22. **(a)** Cytomegalovirus is one of the six types of herpes virus. It can be transmitted sexually or nonsexually, causing symptoms similar to those of mononucleosis: swollen glands, exhaustion, and fever. Cytomegalovirus seems to be epidemic in most countries; according to one source, it is dormant in 65% of adults in the United States. In healthy adults, the disease will usually remain dormant and asymptomatic. However, it is passed from mother to fetus in the womb or during delivery, and once the virus invades the body cells, it can do great damage, enlarging the liver and spleen, causing jaundice, blindness, and retardation. Cytomegalovirus is also a serious health threat in AIDS patients. Often these patients have had the virus lying dormant in their bodies for years, but when their immune systems are weakened, cytomegalovirus is activated, causing pneumonia, blindness, gastric inflammation, and encephalitis.

23. **(d)** Three out of four women will suffer from a yeast infection at some time during their lives. Yeast infections are caused by an overabundance of the fungus *Candida albicans*, or monilia, in the vagina. The fungus is found in the vaginas of many healthy women and in the intestines of both men and women, but when the body's sugar, hormone, or bacteria levels are unbalanced, or when the immune system is suppressed, the fungus can cause symptoms of itching and burning and a discharge from the vagina. In AIDS patients, whose immune systems are damaged, the organism will often cause an infection of the mouth and throat called thrush. While yeast is not usually transmitted sexually, it can infect uncircumcised men and thus be given to a female sexual partner. Treatments include antifungal creams and suppositories, some of which can now be purchased without a prescription. Home remedies, such as insertion of yogurt into the vagina, can provide relief from symptoms but will rarely cure the condition.

24. **(a)** As of 1991, the only pathways discovered for transmittal of the HIV virus are through the blood, semen, or vaginal fluids of an infected person. The following are activities that place you at high risk for acquiring AIDS: having sex (penile-vaginal, penile-anal, or oral) with an infected person; injecting drugs with a needle used by an infected person; or receiving blood, blood products, or semen from an infected donor. If you have casual contact — including hugging, kissing without exchange of saliva, sharing utensils, and so on — with an infected person, you will not get AIDS, nor will you by donating blood or through contact with pets or insects.

25. **(c)** Chlamydia is an STD caused by a bacterium, *Chlamydia trachomatis*. Between 3 and 4 million people a year contract the disease, which can infect the vagina, cervix, Fallopian tubes, uterus, or urethra. Often, chlamydia is asymptomatic, though it can cause discharge and testicular or abdominal pain. It is more often asymptomatic in men than in women. Its "silent" development is the reason for its prevalence; unless it is detected by culture or blood test, many people do not know they are infected and pass the disease on to others. Chlamydia is treated with antibiotics.

26. **(d)** Molluscum contagiosum is caused by a virus and can be spread by sexual contact or sharing of clothing. It causes bumps on the infected areas of skin that can itch and are highly contagious. This disease, often called "the pox," is treated with topical ointments or liquid nitrogen.

27. **(b)** Genital herpes is an infection caused by the herpes simplex virus (HSV-II). It is not curable at present and is transmitted through unprotected sexual activity. Usually, the first outbreak of herpes is the worst: symptoms can include swollen glands, fever, headache, painful urination, vaginal discharge, pain in the legs, and the development of painful blisters, which can appear on the penis, vagina, anus, or cervix. In most cases, herpes recurs, often when the sufferer is under stress or has other health problems. The virus is easily transmitted as long as the blisters remain and during the period known as the "prodromal," when tingling and burning sensations are felt where the blisters will appear. At present, the most effective treatment for HSV-II is acyclovir, taken in ointment form to soothe the blisters or orally to lessen the severity of outbreaks.

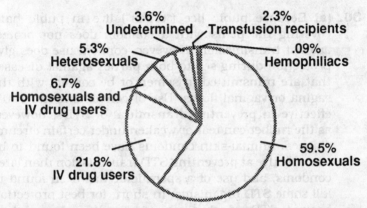

28. (a) According to the November 30, 1990, statistics from the Centers for Disease Control, there are a total of 154,791 Americans with AIDS. Of these, 92,049 are homosexual men, 33,694 are intravenous drug users, 10,356 are homosexual and IV drug users, 3,624 are transfusion recipients, 1,360 are hemophiliacs, 8,204 are heterosexuals, and 5,504 are in an undetermined risk group. The CDC estimates that there are one million people infected with the HIV virus worldwide, and that by the end of 1993 there will be 390,000 to 480,000 Americans with full-blown AIDS, and 285,000 to 340,000 will have died from AIDS.

29. (c) Pelvic inflammatory disease (PID) is an infection of the Fallopian tubes, ovaries, and uterus, usually caused by bacterial STDs such as gonorrhea and chlamydia. If acute, the disease can cause abdominal pain, fever, and discharge and can require hospitalization. "Silent" PID, most often chlamydia-caused, with mild or no symptoms, can cause scarring of the reproductive tract, which in turn can lead to ectopic pregnancy, infertility, and chronic pain. PID is treated with antibiotics and rest, but often treatment cannot prevent the scarring that results in infertility. Use of the IUD has been determined to increase the likelihood of PID, as the bacteria can move up the IUD string and into the uterus.

30. **(a)** Because pubic lice ("crabs") live in pubic hair, covering the penis with a condom does not protect against transmission. However, condom use does give protection during sex to both parties against diseases that are transmitted in semen or by contact with the vagina or vaginal fluids. Use of condoms is not 100% effective in preventing transmittal of STDs, however, as the rubber can tear or weaken under certain circumstances. Animal-skin condoms have been found to be less effective at preventing STD transmission than latex condoms, and use of a spermicide has been found to kill some STD organisms. In short, for best protection against STDs during sex, you and/or your partner should use a condom lubricated with spermicide during penile-oral, -genital, and -anal intercourse. The condom should be put on before pre-ejaculatory fluid appears and before there is any contact with the genitals. If one partner has herpes, the condom must cover all blisters to be effective. For more information on safer sex, see question 34.

31. **(b)** New evidence has linked chlamydia in men to infertility, possibly because the disease can cause blockage of the epididymis, making sperm passage impossible. The same holds true with gonorrhea and nongonococcal urethritis. Although these diseases are more likely to cause infertility in women than in men, they do put men at risk as well, making early diagnosis and treatment important for both sexes.

32. (c) Granuloma inguinale, also known as Donovanosis, is a bacterially-caused STD that is common in Asia and the Caribbean. Only about 100 cases a year are diagnosed in the United States. The initial symptom is a series of raised red sores, appearing on the vulva, cervix, anus, or glans, which can become painful, bleed, or give off pus. Lymph nodes swell, and scarring can occur. The disease is treated with antibiotics.

33. (b) Lesbians are not a group at high risk for contracting AIDS, but there are reported cases of HIV-positive lesbians. Most of these women were IV drug users, but lesbians are also at risk in the same circumstances as the general female population: by having unsafe sex with gay or bisexual men; by using untested donor insemination; and by undergoing blood transfusion. In December 1986, a case of HIV transmission from woman to woman was reported. The initial contact was an IV drug user; her lover had had sex with three men, including one bisexual, so in this case and in the few other reported cases, the route of transmission is not certain. Despite their low risk, lesbians find that the AIDS epidemic affects them in many ways, from the need to practice safer sex to the loss of friends from the disease to the increase in homophobia as a result of the disease.

34. (a) Safer sex (called "safer" because few sexual practices provide 100% protection against STDs) includes those practices in which the risk of acquiring an STD for either partner is very low. Use of condoms on men and dental dams (latex sheets that cover the vulva) on women lower the possibility of infection. Dry kissing is considered safe, as is masturbation (provided hands are free of open cuts or sores), touching, and sharing fantasies. Intercourse with a condom and wet or French kissing are somewhat less safe, and unprotected oral sex or intercourse, fisting (putting a hand into the partner's rectum or vagina), and rimming (anal-oral contact) are considered unsafe practices. While some people feel that the practice of safer sex takes the excitement out of the sexual act, others find that practicing safer sex allows them to free their imaginations and spend more time exploring their sexuality with their partners.

35. (d) Syphilis appears in three stages. In the first stage, the symptoms include a sore (chancre) at the site of infection and swollen lymph nodes. Without treatment, the sore then heals, and after one to twenty-four weeks, the second stage begins, signalled by a rash, often itchy, and sometimes patches of gray sores on mucous membranes, as well as large pink growths on membrane and lymph node sites. These can be accompanied by fever, weight loss, and hair loss, and can last or recur for years. After the second stage, the disease can become latent, to reappear as second stage infection again and again or to remain asymptomatic. The third stage of untreated syphilis can include blindness, mental disorders, heart problems, nerve damage, paralysis, and death.

36. (a) There are dozens of strains of human papilloma virus, the causative agent of genital warts, several of which have been linked to the development of cancer of the cervix, vulva, vagina, penis, and anus. Infection with the HIV virus is thought to lead to Kaposi's sarcoma, a type of skin cancer.

37. (d) A mother infected with gonorrhea can infect her child during birth, causing blindness. Untreated syphilis can infect a fetus, resulting in heart defects, bone deformities, and other ailments after birth. Mothers with AIDS infect their offspring at least 39% of the time, according to the *New England Journal of Medicine.* Many other STDs are transmitted from mother to child, including cytomegalovirus, herpes, condyloma, and chlamydia. These diseases can cause various infections or birth defects in newborns.

38. (b) Enteric pathogens are organisms that affect the intestinal tract, causing fever and diarrhea. They are transmitted as STDs by oral-anal contact and are most frequently diagnosed in homosexual men. These diseases include shigellosis, campylobacter, amebiasis, and giardiasis. They can also be transmitted nonsexually through contaminated food or water.

39. **(c)** A mycoplasma is a bacterium without cell walls. Mycoplasma STDs are a relatively new phenomenon, but are becoming more common. The infection usually follows the same course as chlamydia: it can be silent or cause cervicitis and ascend to the upper reproductive tract to cause PID (see question 29). Scarring is not usually as widespread as that following chlamydia-caused PID, and diagnosis and treatment of mycoplasma follows the same course as that for chlamydia.

40. **(d)** It is possible for most STDs to be transmitted during oral sex, through semen, vaginal fluids, or blood. Use of a condom when oral sex is performed on a man or a dental dam when performed on a woman lowers the possibility of infection. Specialists are divided on the question of whether AIDS can be transmitted through oral sex, but uncertainty on this matter makes unprotected oral sex with an infected partner high-risk behavior.

Sacred and Profane: Licit and Illicit Sex

It doesn't matter what you do, as long as you don't do it in public and frighten the horses.

— MRS. PATRICK CAMPBELL

1. What is the subject of the cases *Roe* v. *Wade* and *Webster* v. *Reproductive Health Services*?

   a. birth control failure

   b. child sexual abuse

   c. abortion

   d. homosexual intercourse

2. In which of these places is same-sex marriage legal?

   a. District of Columbia

   b. Greece

   c. California

   d. Denmark

3. Which of these states does *not* punish adultery with criminal penalties?

   a. Arkansas

   b. New York

   c. California

   d. North Dakota

4. Surrogate motherhood is legal

   a. in some states

   b. in no state

   c. in all states

   d. only when a reasonable sum of money is paid to the birth mother

5. What is the term for one who derives sexual satisfaction from watching others engage in sexual acts?

   a. pictophiliac

   b. catamite

   c. demi-vièrge

   d. voyeur

6. From what does an erotolaliac derive sexual satisfaction?

    a. sex with minors

    b. phone sex

    c. sex in enclosed spaces

    d. violent sex

7. What is another term for pandering?

    a. prostitution

    b. scotophilia

    c. rape

    d. pimping

8. Which of the following is a legal punishment for the crime of rape in the United States?

    a. death

    b. castration

    c. loss of voting rights

    d. all of the above

9. As of June 1991, the Immigration and Naturalization Service is allowed to test immigrants for AIDS

    a. when they are from Africa

    b. under no circumstances

    c. when they are homosexual men

    d. when they visit prostitutes in the United States

10. Why were so many lawsuits brought against the A.H. Robins Company?

    a. Its CEO made obscene phone calls to female mayors across the country.

    b. It manufactured an IUD that caused many deaths.

   c. It manufactured a birth control pill that did not prevent pregnancy.

   d. It encouraged discrimination against female employees.

11. Which of the following is considered a fetish?

   a. arousal by fondling children's genitals

   b. arousal by watching a striptease

   c. arousal by handling leather

   d. all of the above

12. How many women are estimated to be the victims of domestic violence in the United States each year?

   a. 40,000

   b. 400,000

   c. 4 million

   d. 40 million

13. Legally, a child infected with HIV can go to school

   a. if he or she is kept away from other children

   b. under any circumstances

   c. only before full-blown AIDS develops

   d. only if no one knows of the infection

14. Where is the public use of obscene language a crime?

   a. in most states

   b. in no state

   c. in Alabama only

   d. in all states

15. In which of these countries is homosexuality illegal?

    a. Australia

    b. Israel

    c. Ireland

    d. all of the above

16. In which state is incest legal?

    a. California

    b. Kansas

    c. New York

    d. none of the above

17. What did the LaRouche Initiative of 1986 propose?

    a. resettlement camps for all homosexuals

    b. the death penalty for convicted sex offenders

    c. quarantining of people with AIDS in California

    d. dismissal of homosexuals working in health or food services

18. What constitutes statutory rape?

    a. rape that violates a national statute

    b. rape of a male by a male or female

    c. rape that involves transportation across state lines

    d. intercourse with a minor

19. Approximately how many children are victims of sexual abuse in the United States each year?

    a. 2,000

    b. 20,000

    c. 200,000

    d. 2 million

20. What is zooeroticism?

    a. sex in a zoo

    b. sex with animals

    c. masturbation while looking at pictures of animals

    d. sex while wearing animal products such as leather or wool

21. More than 30% of all acts of voyeurism and incest take place

    a. while the perpetrator is drunk

    b. in middle-class homes

    c. between consenting adults

    d. in public

22. In which of these states is sodomy legal?

    a. Alabama, Florida, and Georgia

    b. Missouri, Oklahoma, and Virginia

    c. Maryland, Michigan, and Rhode Island

    d. Iowa, Nebraska, and North Dakota

23. What does a cock ring do?

    a. It tickles the vagina, causing pleasurable sensations.

    b. It helps a man to retain his erection.

    c. In masturbation, it serves as a receptacle for semen.

    d. It is merely decorative.

24. *Justine* and *Venus in Furs* are classic tales of

    a. sadomasochism

    b. child molestation

    c. prostitution

    d. men living as women

25. The 1986 ruling in *Bowers* v. *Hardwick* concluded that

    a. sex between consenting adults is protected under law

    b. homosexuals must be treated equally in the workplace

    c. the law does not protect couples who engage in oral sex in their own homes

    d. Georgia's sodomy laws are unconstitutional

26. In which of the following places is prostitution illegal?

    a. France

    b. England

    c. Japan

    d. Nevada

27. Blood tests to prove paternity are accurate to within

    a. 20 to 25%

    b. 45 to 50%

    c. 90 to 95%

    d. 99 to 100%

28. In order to be legally obscene, visual material must

    a. appeal to a prurient interest in sex

    b. offend community standards

    c. lack literary, artistic, political, or scientific value

    d. all of the above

29. A person, other than the prostitute or a child of the prostitute or legal dependent incapable of self-support, who is supported in whole or in substantial part by the proceeds of prostitution is a

    a. pimp

    b. concubine

    c. harlot

    d. charlatan

30. A pedophile gets sexual fulfillment from encounters with

    a. shoes

    b. pets

    c. older women

    d. children

31. Why did a Los Angeles couple's death in a plane crash in Chile cause trouble in Australia?

    a. The couple, two men married in a civil ceremony in Chile, were on an Australian airline that did not recognize their marriage.

    b. At the time of the crash, the couple was engaged in a sexual act with members of the Australian "Mile High Club."

    c. The couple failed to leave instructions in their will about what to do with their embryos, orphaned in a freezer in an Australian clinic.

    d. The Chilean government refused to release the body of the man, who was wanted for sex crimes in Brisbane, Australia.

32. Can you be prosecuted for giving someone the HIV virus?

    a. No, but there is a movement to make it illegal.

    b. No, it is impossible to prove willful intent.

    c. Yes, if you live in Florida or Idaho.

    d. Yes, willful exposure is against the law.

33. Among men arrested for sex crimes, most are arrested for

    a. pedophilia

    b. rape

    c. exhibitionism

    d. soliciting

34. A gigolo is

    a. any man who sells sex

    b. a heterosexual man who sells sex to women

    c. a woman or man who sells sex to an older member of the opposite sex

    d. a male street hustler

35. Until 1971, gays and lesbians working for the federal government were

    a. summarily dismissed

    b. subject to periodic psychiatric examinations

    c. routinely tested for drugs

    d. relegated to menial positions

36. Approximately half of all rape victims

    a. know their rapist

    b. are dressed provocatively at the time of the attack

    c. are attacked after midnight

    d. are men

37. A victim of frotteurism may
   a. be relieved of her clothing at gunpoint
   b. have a stranger press against her on the subway
   c. be subjected to obscene phone calls
   d. be forced to pose nude

38. A transvestite may be arrested for
   a. engaging in sex with a woman
   b. soliciting sex for money
   c. wearing women's clothing in public
   d. all of the above

39. In which states was marriage between whites and blacks still illegal in 1966?
   a. Alabama, Mississippi, and South Carolina
   b. Arkansas, Florida, and Kentucky
   c. Oklahoma, Texas, and West Virginia
   d. all of the above

40. In 1990, a woman sued a fertility clinic for
   a. giving her husband's sperm to another woman
   b. substituting another man's sperm for her husband's
   c. accidentally melting her frozen embryos
   d. refusing to implant her with her cousin's sperm

TEST 7: Explanatory Answers

1. **(c)** In 1973, the case *Roe* v. *Wade* reached the Supreme Court. The case concerned a woman, known as Jane Roe, and her right to have an abortion. The Supreme Court ruled that a woman had the right to abort in the first trimester of pregnancy, linking this right with the right to privacy. States were give the right to have a say in abortions performed from the third to the sixth month of pregnancy. In 1989, *Webster* v. *Reproductive Health Services* upheld states' rights to ban abortions that would use tax money, except where such a procedure would save a woman's life. *Roe* v. *Wade* has recently been challenged in the Supreme Court, but as of this writing it is still law, though states have passed laws requiring minors to have parental approval for abortion, and several states have considered the father's right to stop an abortion.

2. **(d)** In 1990, Craig Dean and Patrick Gill applied for a marriage license in Washington, DC. The license was denied to them on the grounds that the District of Columbia Code did not allow marriage between persons of the same sex. In fact, there is no state or area in the United States in which same-sex marriage is legal, and in the rest of the world, only Denmark has legalized it.

3. **(a)** There are few states that do not offer criminal penalties for adultery; among them are Arkansas, Louisiana, and Nevada. The law is about to be challenged in Connecticut. States have varying interpretations of the offense: for example, in South Carolina, if adulterers do not live together, adultery must be "habitual" to be punished. Punishments also vary widely, from a fine of ten dollars to five years in jail. Often, the laws on adultery only come into play when divorce is an issue, as it is nearly a universal reason for divorce.

4. **(a)** In the "Baby M" case, a New Jersey couple, the Sterns, hired Mary Beth Whitehead to bear their child for $10,000. The birth mother changed her mind after

giving birth, and the couple sued for custody. The state Supreme Court found in favor of Whitehead, ruling that surrogacy was legal as long as money was not paid directly to the birth mother and she voluntarily gives up her child. However, other factors in the case led to a custody hearing that placed Baby M with the Sterns. Louisiana is one state that has banned surrogacy outright; others have followed New Jersey's lead in allowing it with the birth mother's consent.

5. **(d)** Voyeurs, or Peeping Toms, need to watch others to achieve sexual stimulation. They will rarely watch people they know well, preferring novelty and risk to heighten the experience. Usually voyeurism is classified as a misdemeanor; often, states attempt to include treatment by a psychiatrist or social worker with the punishment. Legend has it that the original Peeping Tom disobeyed an order not to look out the window when Lady Godiva rode by naked on her horse; he was struck blind as a punishment.

6. **(b)** Erotolaliacs receive stimulation from talking about sex or listening to talk about sex. They often find an outlet for their aberration by making obscene telephone calls. Often, erotolaliacs are also coprolaliacs — that is, they need to use obscene language for stimulation. In a recent case, a university president harassed a woman with obscene telephone calls, and claimed his erotolalia began as a result of remembering childhood sexual abuse. Obscenity over the telephone is a misdemeanor in many states, invoking a penalty of from $100 and 30 days in jail to $5,000 and/or two years in jail.

7. **(d)** By law, pandering is defined as procuring a female for a house of prostitution, whether or not she gives her consent. The law includes means of procurement such as promises, tricks, threats, or force. The crime is a felony in many cases, and the punishments can be very high, especially when pandering is forcible or takes place across state lines.

8. **(d)** Rape is legally defined as sexual intercourse with a woman without her consent. The wording of the definition raises a problem: the determination of "consent." Some courts have considered the failure to object as consent. Others have had to draw up specific statutes addressing rape of the mentally handicapped, where consent cannot be determined. Rape is a felony in all states; many people advocate life imprisonment or the death penalty on conviction. In several states, including South Carolina and Michigan, under certain circumstances, the offender can be castrated either surgically or by drugs, though arguments against this punishment are ongoing because many claim it violates the Eighth Amendment and is cruel and unusual punishment. According to *Sexual Conduct and the Law*, in South Carolina, Tennessee, and New Jersey a conviction brings about revocation of voting rights. In 1989, there were 94,504 reported incidences of rape. Regionally, the West has the highest incidence, with 83 rapes per 100,000 females; the South is next, then the Midwest, then the Northeast.

9. **(b)** The laws of immigration to the United States exclude any alien afflicted with a dangerous contagious disease on a list determined by the Office of Health and Human Services. Up until 1991, this included AIDS. Immigrants were not tested as they entered, but if the INS or the consular office had reason to believe an immigrant was infected, they could test that person. This practice was open to abuse; for example, recently a Dutch health administrator traveled to the United States with informative pamphlets about AIDS, and was forced to get tested in order to enter the country. In 1990, a law was passed that allows the Secretary of Health and Human Services to remove any disease from the list of those that prevent entry, and early in 1991 AIDS was removed from the list. However, the reinstatement of AIDS on the list is currently under dispute.

10. **(b)** The A.H. Robins Company manufactured the Dalkon Shield, an IUD that resulted in a large number of

cases of pelvic inflammatory disease and at least 17 deaths due to septic miscarriages. There have been 1,570 lawsuits against the company, which is in bankruptcy. The manufacturer of the Copper-7 IUD, G.D. Searle, has had 800 lawsuits brought against it. Because of this, most IUD manufacturers have stopped production; only two kinds of IUD are now available in the United States.

11. **(c)** A fetish is defined as the need to use a particular item in a sexual act to achieve arousal. Fetish items can include shoes, leather, women's underwear, and human excrement. Photographs of fetish items are often enough for arousal, but some fetishists must collect or steal the item they desire to achieve stimulation. Fetish items that are considered by many to be acceptable include women's breasts and other body parts; others, such as diapers or urine, are considered deviant.

12. **(c)** Although much domestic violence goes unreported, estimated figures are alarmingly high, and women have a great deal of trouble getting protection or legal help with the problem. Until the 1870s, wife abuse was legal, and it continues to be difficult to prove. Women who are victims of abuse are advised to leave the domestic situation, report it to a physician and to the police, swear out a complaint, and get an order of protection. Rarely will the spouse or lover end up in jail, even if he violates the order. In some states, when a husband and wife live together, the man cannot be accused of raping his wife. However, as domestic violence escalates, or as better reporting of it raises national awareness, states are beginning to change this law. Of course, domestic violence is not only enacted against women; there have been cases reported involving men beaten by their spouses or lovers, too.

13. **(b)** All of the court cases that have so far addressed the issue of schoolchildren with AIDS have eventually ended by granting the child in question the right to attend school. The best-known of these cases concerned Ryan

White, an Indiana boy afflicted with hemophilia who developed AIDS in 1984. His school board tried to prevent his attendance at school; the court barred him, but the family transferred the case to another district and the ban was overturned. The Centers for Disease Control have recommended that each case be evaluated separately, and that those children who are very young or neurologically impaired, and who might not have control of their body fluids, be kept in a more controlled environment.

14. **(a)** Public expression of obscene language or obscenity is a misdemeanor in most states, though some have rather unusual grounds for making it a crime. In many states it is a crime if it disturbs religious meetings or occurs on public transportation. In Minnesota it is a crime if done in a dance hall. In California a funeral director who voices obscenity can be disciplined; in Massachusetts an embalmer who uses obscenity can be dismissed. Recently, the town of Quincy, Massachusetts, made obscenity a crime under any circumstances; the American Civil Liberties Union is considering challenging this ruling on the grounds that it interferes with freedom of speech.

15. **(d)** Homosexuality is against the law in the countries listed as well as Algeria, Chile, China, Cuba, Egypt, India, Iran, Libya, Mexico, Morocco, Mozambique, Nigeria, Pakistan, Rumania, South Africa, the Soviet Union, Tanzania, Tunisia, and Uruguay. Iran and Chile routinely torture and execute gays; the Soviet criminal code forbids being a homosexual, whether or not one engages in homosexual sex.

16. **(d)** Incest is illegal in all states and is banned in nearly all countries and cultures. In fact, 32 states consider marriages between first cousins illegal and prohibit them. The penalties for incest range from at least one year and/or a fine of $500 in South Carolina to life imprisonment for incestuous rape of young children in

Washington, Ohio, and Oregon. In Tennessee, if a man impregnates his sister-in-law, he receives a 10-year sentence; in North Carolina if an uncle commits incest with a niece or an aunt with a nephew, the crime is only a misdemeanor. It is estimated that 10 to 20 million people in the United States have been victims or perpetrators of incest; these relationships cut across class and economic lines.

17. **(c)** Lyndon LaRouche, a right-wing extremist, proposed in California an initiative requiring testing of all California residents and quarantining of everyone who came into contact with HIV. The initiative was endorsed by many and appeared on the ballot, but was defeated. Other such measures have been proposed, and discrimination against AIDS sufferers continues in the workplace, schools, insurance, health care, housing, the military, and in funeral homes. (In New York, funeral homes that refuse the bodies of AIDS victims can be prosecuted.) Discrimination even exists after embalming: some cemeteries will not bury people who have died from the disease.

18. **(d)** Statutory rape does not require force to be considered rape, nor does it hinge on the victim's consent. The laws concerning statutory rape are formulated to protect minors, so consent is immaterial. If, however, a minor is raped using force and against her will, the crime will usually be prosecuted as rape. In some states, it is considered statutory rape for a woman to have sex with a male minor, but usually the crime victim is female. Penalties range from death for rape of victims under 12 to discretionary sterilization and imprisonment to long jail terms. The age of consent varies from state to state; in Delaware it is 7; in other states 14, 16, or 18.

19. **(c)** Child sexual abuse is a crime in every state and receives more public attention each year. The crime,

when perpetrated against very young children, is often hard to prove, as young children rarely give reliable testimony. Evidence in these cases can include testimony from a child as young as three years, medical examinations, evidence of prior offenses, and evidence of opportunity for abuse. When such abuse is perpetrated by a parent (usually the father), a child protection proceeding can also be enacted against the passive parent. Child sex offenders are usually victims of personality disorders and have histories of alienation, dysfunctional relationships, and difficulty controlling impulses.

20. **(b)** Zooeroticism, or zoophilia, is the practice of having sex with an animal. More than 15% of boys who live on farms, according to the research of Alfred Kinsey (1948, 1953), have had sex with animals. Fewer women than men practice bestiality. Bestiality has been around for centuries; Governor William Bradford of Plymouth Colony reported incidents of zoophilia in his journals. In common law, bestiality was considered a crime against nature and was punishable by death; now, in all states but New Hampshire, zoophilia is a felony.

21. **(a)** Alcohol is a contributing factor in a very high percentage of sex crimes. In *Sex: The Facts, the Acts and Your Feelings*, the author cites a study that shows that 66.7% of heterosexual sex crimes against children take place under the influence. Incest against children involves alcohol 30.8% of the time, and 30.7% of exhibitionists are intoxicated when they commit their crime.

22. **(d)** By definition, sodomy (named for the homosexual practices popular in the Biblical city of Sodom) includes these acts: intercourse with a member of the same sex or with an animal, anal sex with a member of either sex, and oral sex with a member of either sex. In United States law, it refers to any act of oral-genital or anal-genital sex. At this writing, sodomy is legal in only 26 states: Alaska, California, Colorado, Connecticut, Del-

SACRED AND PROFANE: LICIT AND ILLICIT SEX

aware, Hawaii, Illinois, Indiana, Iowa, Maine, Massachusetts, Nebraska, New Hampshire, New Jersey, New Mexico, New York, North Dakota, Ohio, Oregon, Pennsylvania, South Dakota, Vermont, Washington, West Virginia, Wisconsin, and Wyoming. In all other states and the District of Columbia, sodomy laws are still on the books, although in Arkansas, Kansas, Montana, Nevada, and Texas, the law applies *only* to acts between people of the same sex.

23. **(b)** Sex aids may be just for pleasure, as with scented oils, French ticklers, or ben wa balls, or they may actually provide assistance in the act itself. Cock rings fit around the erect penis and put pressure on the veins, keeping the penis engorged and prolonging the erection. Sex aids are rarely illegal and are usually easy to find — vibrators and massage oils are routinely sold through the mail, for example.

24. **(a)** The term *sadomasochism* derives from the names of the authors of these works. Donatien Alphonse François, comte de Sade, better known as the Marquis de Sade (1740–1814), wrote books deemed pornographic during several of his prison terms for sexual abuses in the late 1700s (*Justine*, 1791). His writings are part novel, part tract, embracing the principles of what is now called *sadism*: the erotic domination of a partner through infliction of physical pain. Leopold von Sacher-Masoch (1836–1895), an Austrian novelist writing a century later, filled his books with depictions of his own favorite pastime: submitting to physical and mental punishment by a lover, now called *masochism*. Both men were heterosexual. There are many types of sadomasochism; one popular form is bondage & discipline, in which one partner is tied up and is "punished" by the other.

25. **(c)** In 1982, a police officer appeared at Michael Hardwick's home to serve him with a warrant dealing with a charge of public intoxication. The officer was let in,

whereupon he observed Michael Hardwick engaging in oral sex with another man. The men were arrested under Georgia's sodomy laws, and the ensuing court battles became a test of citizens' rights to privacy. Hardwick challenged his arrest (*Bowers* is the name of the Georgia Attorney General), and the case went up to the U.S. Court of Appeals, which declared Georgia sodomy laws unconstitutional. The state then appealed, and the case wound up in Supreme Court. In 1986, the Court ruled that there is no protection guaranteed in the Constitution for acts of sodomy between adults in their own homes. The Court thus refused to strike down local sodomy laws (see question 22).

26. **(c)** Prostitution, the selling of sexual favors, was legal throughout the United States until the Mann Act of 1910 banned transportation of women across state lines for immoral purposes and a series of 1915 laws outlawed brothels. Only in Nevada is it now legal to sell sex, and prostitutes in Nevada are issued ID cards to make the business easier to control. In England and France, as in many countries in Europe, prostitution is legal, although open soliciting is not. Japan outlawed prostitution in 1957. For more on the world's oldest profession, see Test 8.

27. **(d)** There are three main blood tests for paternity, and they can be combined to provide accuracy of close to 100%. Generally, paternity suits come about when a mother wishes to receive monetary child support and the man she names as the father doubts her word. The tests compare genetic markers in the blood of the child and the probable father. DNA "fingerprinting" is even more precise and may eventually replace these blood tests.

28. **(d)** With a vague definition like this the standard against which to judge, it is no wonder that pornography cases are nearly impossible to prosecute. Pornography can be in the form of erotic writings, lewd pictures, X-rated

films, or even anatomically-correct statuary, depending on your definition. United States obscenity laws are based in part on the British Obscene Publications Act of 1857, which failed to define obscenity. The 1865 Mail Act and the Comstock Law of 1873 made it illegal to mail or receive "lewd" and "lascivious" publications, which at that time included information on birth control. The 1934 case *United States* v. *One Book Entitled Ulysses* referred to "libidinous effect" as a means of determining obscenity. (*Ulysses* was not found to be obscene.) In 1957's *Roth* v. *United States*, the Court referred for the first time to "contemporary community standards" and appeal to "prurient interests." In *"Memoirs"* v. *Massachusetts*, a 1966 case involving the novel *Fanny Hill*, the Court spoke of a work "utterly without redeeming social value." (*Fanny Hill* was not found to be obscene.) Redeeming social value, prurient interest, and community standards continued to be the key to judgments until *Miller* v. *California* (1973), wherein "social value" was changed to "serious literary, artistic, political, or scientific value." The 1973 decision reaffirmed the notion that pornography is not protected by laws protecting free speech. Of course, the classic comment on the issue is that of Justice Potter Stewart in his concurring opinion for *Jacobellis* v. *Ohio* (1964): "I shall not today attempt to further define the kinds of material. . . but I know it when I see it."

29. **(a)** This is the legal definition of a pimp, although certain laws also refer to anyone who solicits clients for a prostitute or who transports someone across state lines for purposes of prostitution. Most pimps are men, and they may have a single prostitute working for them or oversee a stable of prostitutes. In return for a sizeable percentage of a prostitute's fee, a pimp may supply shelter, drugs, and/or bail money.

30. **(d)** Genuine pedophiles prefer sex with children over sex with adults. Pedophiles used to be the object of jokes and snickering, but recent revelations about the extent of child molestation have changed society's attitude. Almost all pedophiles are men or teenaged boys, and most who act out their pedophilia do so by attempting to seduce young girls. Occasionally, pedophiles are homosexual men who are attracted to young boys. Almost no incidents of female pedophilia have been recorded. Every state in the Union considers active pedophilia a criminal offense. The North American Man-Boy Love Association (NAMBLA) grew out of a defense fund for men in Boston accused of having sex with young teens.

31. **(c)** The moral of the story is that you should consider your embryos part of your property when you make out your will, or risk embroiling them in court cases for years. Mario and Elsa Rios, having tried other routes to fertility, had traveled to Australia, the home of radical new techniques of in vitro fertilization, and had fertilized some embryos for later implantation. The embryos were then frozen, and were in that state when the couple was killed in 1983. On September 4, 1984, a panel of distinguished judges, theologians, scientists, and philosophers recommended the destruction of the embryos; but on October 24, lawmakers overturned the decision and called for the embryos to be implanted in surrogate mothers and placed for adoption. By December 5, 1987, nothing had yet been done, and the Victoria state government finally ruled that the embryos should be thawed and implanted in an infertile Australian woman, with the clear understanding that there was no way of knowing whether embryos frozen so long would still be viable.

32. **(c)** As of this writing, Idaho and Florida are the only states that call willful and knowing transmission of HIV a crime, but other states are considering it. A number of lawsuits have arisen from transmission of STDs including AIDS; the standard claim, according to Gail Koff in *Love and the Law*, is negligence or unlawful

battery. The plaintiff must prove that the defendant knew he or she was infected and proceeded to transmit the disease anyway.

33. **(c)** Exhibitionists apparently thrill to the revulsion of their victims. Exhibitionists expose their genitals to others, usually strangers, and may or may not masturbate while flashing. Only very rarely is an exhibitionist violent or dangerous.

34. **(b)** Gigolos (from the French *gigolette*, meaning "dance-hall pick-up") are men who perform sexual services for women. They may also serve as social escorts. Generally they are not streetwalkers but are more like call girls—more expensive and upscale than hustlers. A gigolo may be "kept" by a woman, or he may have several clients at once. Like other forms of prostitution, this one is illegal in 49 states and the District of Columbia.

35. **(a)** Needless to say, this policy kept many gay and lesbian federal employees in the closet. Until 1972 and 1973 respectively, the National Association of Social Workers and the American Psychiatric Association considered homosexuality a disease, which aided those who would discriminate against gays and lesbians. With the psychiatric stigma removed, discrimination has been based primarily on sodomy laws, and states that retain these laws tend to make it harder than others for gays and lesbians to adopt children, gain custody, inherit a lover's property, teach school, and so on. Since no federal policy exists, cases tend to be decided one at a time locally, based to varying extent on community standards and state laws.

36. **(a)** Rapes are historically underreported crimes—perhaps over 90% are never reported—and one reason may be the high incidence of acquaintance rapes. In such cases, the defendent usually claims that the victim consented to intercourse, and prosecution may be difficult unless the victim sustained visible injuries or a witness was present. Victims increase their likelihood of successful prosecution if they report the crime immediately. Date rapes are more common on and around college campuses than anywhere else, and many universities have programs designed to educate women and men about the crime. Marital rape is even more difficult to prosecute; at this writing only Oregon, New Jersey, and Delaware allow a wife to charge her husband with rape; other states do not concede that nonconsensual intercourse is always rape even when it takes place between husband and wife.

37. (b) *Frotter* is French for "to rub," and *frottage* may refer to the art of pencil rubbing or to something a bit more aberrant—the act of rubbing against a stranger for sexual pleasure. Frotteurism is a form of sexual assault, but it is rarely reported because it is usually a fleeting and anonymous encounter in a crowd.

38. (b) Cross-dressing by itself is not against the law, but prostitution is, and the occasional gay transvestite who dresses in women's clothing to solicit sex from other men can be arrested for solicitation.

39. (d) The term *miscegenation*, referring to a mixing of the races, was apparently coined in 1864 by David Goodman Croly, a journalist and pamphleteer. In 1958, Richard Loving, a white man, married Mildred Jeter, a black and American Indian woman. They lived in Washington, DC, for some time, but upon moving to Virginia, they were prosecuted under that state's miscegenation law and sentenced to one year in jail, to be suspended if they left the state. They refused to leave and appealed the verdict. When the case reached the Supreme Court in 1967, the Court overturned all miscegenation laws, affecting all of the states listed in a, b, and c, as well as Virginia, Delaware, Louisiana, Missouri, North Carolina, and Tennessee. The law had been challenged once before, in 1883, but was upheld then because it was determined that since both whites and blacks could be prosecuted under it, the law was not discriminatory.

40. **(b)** When Julia Skolnick's husband was diagnosed with cancer, he donated his sperm to a sperm bank to protect it from damage from his radiation treatments. In 1986, Ms. Skolnick was impregnated with sperm from the sperm bank; in December, she gave birth to a child. The Skolnicks were white; their child was black. Ms. Skolnick did not take legal action until after her husband's death in 1989, but by that time felt that the "racial taunting" of her child had become "intolerable," and some recourse was required. DNA analysis confirmed that the child was not her husband's, and Ms. Skolnick sued the fertility clinic and sperm bank for malpractice and negligence.

Back to the Garden: Sex in Cultural History

> Our biological drives are several
> million years older than our
> intelligence.
>
> — *ARTHUR E. MORGAN*

1. Giovanni Casanova and Frank Harris achieved fame after
   a. being arrested and jailed for sexual misconduct
   b. publishing memoirs detailing their sexual adventures
   c. pursuing and seducing members of the French court
   d. all of the above

2. Eugenic arguments have traditionally been used to limit
   a. the size of the underclass
   b. the number of girls born to a given family
   c. marriages between distant cousins
   d. the selection of the name *Eugene*

3. *Hetaerae*, *devadasis*, and *ishtaritu* were all names for
   a. sexual rituals
   b. coming-of-age rites
   c. the beloved in the *Kama-sutra*
   d. prostitutes

4. Branding of adulterers was standard punishment in the society built by the
   a. Puritans
   b. Romans
   c. Sumerians
   d. all of the above

5. What was unusual about the Tchambuli people studied by Margaret Mead?
   a. Men and women warred together against other tribes.
   b. The men were passive, and the women ruled.

    c. Women and men shared all jobs equally.

    d. Men became pregnant and gave birth.

6. According to Catholic doctrine, why is abortion so grievous a sin?

    a. It might rid the world of a potential Messiah.

    b. Every child deserves a life dedicated to Christ.

    c. The unbaptized soul of the fetus is condemned to hell.

    d. It directly contradicts the writings of the Apostles.

7. Celibacy for priests and monks became the rule of the Church during the time of

    a. Christ

    b. Saint Augustine (354–430)

    c. Gregory VII (Pope 1073–1085)

    d. Paul III (Pope 1534–1549)

8. Sex during pregnancy is still taboo among strict followers of

    a. Judaism

    b. Islam

    c. Catholicism

    d. all of the above

9. What did Draupadi of the *Mahabharata* and King David of the Bible have in common?

    a. They were both polygamous.

    b. They both kept concubines.

    c. They were both bisexual.

    d. They were both cross-dressers.

10. On what principle did Thomas Aquinas and John Calvin agree with the Talmud?

   a. the separation of Church and state

   b. the infallibility of the Pope

   c. the notion that homosexuality is unnatural

   d. the idea that original sin resides in women

11. UNICEF has called for a worldwide end to

   a. teenage pregnancies

   b. the sterilization of retarded children

   c. prostitution

   d. clitoridectomies

12. How is circumcision as described in the Bible different from circumcision of Polynesians, Aztecs, and dynastic Egyptians?

   a. It may only take place at night.

   b. It is only meant for the upper classes.

   c. Other circumcisions involve the testicles.

   d. It is not a rite of puberty.

13. Which famous mistress is *not* matched correctly with her lover?

   a. Thaïs and Alexander the Great

   b. Diane de Poitiers and Henry IV

   c. Madame Pompadour and Louis XV

   d. Martha Skavronskaya and Peter the Great

14. After a wedding, it was once traditional in many cultures to display

   a. sexually provocative gifts from the wedding guests

   b. pictures of the bride's unmarried sisters

    c. the bloodied sheets from the marriage bed

    d. all of the above

15. Which culture considered menstruating women "unclean"?

    a. Orthodox Jews

    b. Carrier Indians

    c. Victorian English

    d. all of the above

16. Which of the following women was probably exclusively lesbian?

    a. Sappho

    b. George Eliot

    c. Virginia Woolf

    d. Gertrude Stein

17. Why did Onan "spill his seed on the ground"?

    a. He was indulging in self-abuse.

    b. He refused to have intercourse with his brother's wife.

    c. His beloved donkey would not stand still.

    d. He believed that children grew "like weeds."

18. The poet Agathon; Lord Cornbury, colonial governor of New York; and Olympic gold medalist Stella Walsh were all

    a. killed by angry mobs due to their sexual preferences

    b. jailed for sexual abuses

    c. transvestites

    d. authors of pornographic works

19. When was sex education formally introduced in American schools?

   a. 1892

   b. 1932

   c. 1945

   d. 1964

20. Chamberlains in the Courts of Caliphs and certain seventeenth-century opera singers were

   a. eunuchs

   b. lesbians

   c. midwives

   d. gigolos

21. In the twelfth century, the ideal female courtly lover was expected to be

   a. chaste and well-educated

   b. noble and beautiful

   c. devout and unmarried

   d. a mother

22. The harem developed as a result of the religion of

   a. Catholicism

   b. Lutheranism

   c. Islam

   d. Buddhism

23. The fifth-century Indian guide to love and love-making was

   a. the *Kama-sutra*

   b. *The Perfumed Garden*

   c. the *Ars Amatoria*

   d. the *Roman de la Rose*

24. What did the medieval *droit de seigneur* allow?

    a. the keeping of concubines by noblemen

    b. the murder of serf women by noblemen

    c. protection of serf women from abusive husbands

    d. sexual intercourse with vassal brides by noblemen

25. What occurred during the Roman festivals of Bacchus?

    a. Men sought sexual release with holy prostitutes.

    b. Virgins were devoutly relieved of their maidenheads.

    c. All sexual inhibitions were cast off.

    d. Both men and women chose lovers for the coming year.

26. When was it discovered that the ovum played a role in the creation of new life?

    a. the nineteenth century

    b. the eighteenth century

    c. the seventeenth century

    d. the sixteenth century

27. In which of these times and places was homosexuality legal?

    a. Rome in the sixth century

    b. Spain in the sixteenth century

    c. France in the nineteenth century

    d. Chile in the twentieth century

28. Which of the following was once used as birth control?

  a. crocodile dung
  b. lint, honey, and acacia tips
  c. goat bladders
  d. all of the above

29. As a result of the Victorian attitude toward sex,

  a. homosexuality became socially acceptable
  b. prostitution and venereal disease ran rampant
  c. adulterers were put to death
  d. women discovered the pleasures of the sex act

30. What do these figures have in common: Cybele, Astarte, and Demeter?

  a. They were all sacrificed to gods of love.
  b. They were chosen to bear Zeus's children.
  c. They were all goddesses of fertility.
  d. Their followers were all lesbians.

31. Which of these religions considered sex a sacred duty?

  a. Taoism
  b. Calvinism
  c. Confucianism
  d. Islam

32. What was Margaret Sanger's contribution to the history of sexuality?

  a. She studied and wrote on the sexuality of women through the ages.
  b. She opened birth control clinics around the world.

c. She invented the birth control pill.

d. She discovered the role of the clitoris in female orgasm.

33. Where and when did homosexual prostitution flourish?

a. in medieval Germany

b. in thirteenth-century Japan

c. in nineteenth-century Paris

d. in colonial Africa

34. Penis rings were first used in

a. India

b. England

c. America

d. China

(The Granger Collection)

35. This illustration is typical of sexual art from

a. Africa

b. India

   c. Japan

   d. Cincinnati

36. What is the most universally taboo sexual act?

   a. anal sex

   b. oral sex

   c. incest

   d. group sex

37. Who was Sappho?

   a. a French courtesan

   b. a Greek poet

   c. an Indian painter

   d. a Roman goddess

38. What was the act referred to by the French as *le vice anglais*?

   a. flagellation

   b. anal intercourse

   c. French kissing

   d. all of the above

39. What do the following historical figures have in common: Pope Julius III, Somerset Maugham, Alexander the Great, and Christopher Marlowe?

   a. They all frequented prostitutes.

   b. They were all celibate.

   c. They were all homosexuals.

   d. They were all flagellants.

40. What do the following historical figures have in common: Henry VIII, Mussolini, and Christopher Columbus?

   a. They were all homosexuals.

   b. They were all cross-dressers.

c. They were all voyeurs.
d. They all suffered from syphilis.

TEST 8: Explanatory Answers

1. **(b)** Giovanni Jacopo Casanova de Seingalt (1725–1798) was an Italian seminarian in the early 1700s. Expelled from the seminary for sexual misconduct, he began a long tour of Europe, where he lived off his gambling habit and the good graces of his many lovers. He ended his days as a librarian in Bohemia. His autobiography, *Memoires*, was published in 12 volumes nearly 30 years after his death. Frank Harris (1856–1931) was an Irishman who worked in the United States as a journalist and editor of such publications as *Vanity Fair* and *Saturday Review. My Life and Loves*, published in three volumes from 1923 to 1927, was scandalous enough to be banned for years.

2. **(a)** Any historical period of privation, be it in Dickensian England or the South during the Great Depression, has brought with it arguments in favor of eugenics. Eugenics deals with the improvement through breeding techniques of the hereditary qualities of a species— standard operating procedure for horsebreeders or goldfish owners, but raising some important ethical issues when applied to human beings. Eugenics was once based on now-discredited Lamarckian theories of evolution, which stated that environmental changes cause structural changes that can be passed on to offspring. If a man is a drunk, eugenists thought, his children will be drunks, and therefore he should be prevented from having children. In Victorian times, eugenic studies reported that the state of mind of a woman at impregnation would affect her fetus; obviously a poor and hopeless woman would have a deformed or demented child. (Low birth weights due to malnutrition often "proved" this to be true.) The history of eugenics is entangled with the history of birth control; planned children were thought to be of better quality. To limit the poor population has been a goal of politicians and neo-Malthusians alike, but the intent has often been racist as well as elitist. Results have included the eugenic experiments by the Nazis and "Negro Projects" in the

Depression-era South, aimed at convincing black women to cease breeding "carelessly and disastrously" (as cited by Linda Gordon in *Woman's Body, Woman's Right*).

3. **(d)** Perhaps the oldest recorded temple brothel was dedicated to Ishtar, the Assyrian and Babylonian love goddess. Temple prostitutes, ishtaritu, were common in Sumeria and Babylonia, where they brought in money for the upkeep of the temple. They were somewhat less common in Hinduism, but in parts of India, devadasis served the worshippers. The Greek hetaerae were the upper class of Greek prostitutes, usually well-educated and able to converse intelligently on issues of the day. In this they resembled Chinese courtesans, who were also unusually accomplished compared to most women of the time. Lower class streetwalkers existed in all of these societies but were never accorded the respect given to temple prostitutes or hetaerae.

4. **(a)** Puritanism began in England as a movement to reform and purify the Church. Puritans based their beliefs in part on the works of John Calvin (1509–1564), who stated that people are born in sin and must lead holy lives dedicated to God. Paralleling the Puritans' belief in the absolute power of God's will was their strong belief in the absolute power of the male figure in the family. Puritans brought their religious zeal and discipline to America after they were thrown out of the Church of England in 1660. Thanks to their strict laws prohibiting frivolous pleasures or anything that might threaten the family structure, Puritanism is now synonymous with repression.

5. **(b)** Margaret Mead (1901–1978) was an anthropologist whose studies of cultures in the South Pacific helped to discredit the belief that sex roles are fixed and innate. Among the New Guinea peoples she studied were the Tchambuli, a society in which the women fished, engaged in commerce, and ran the household while the men made art, played music, gossiped, and generally

behaved in a way Mead referred to as "moody" and "catty." Mead published these data in her 1935 book *Sex and Temperament in Three Primitive Societies*, in which she also discussed the passive, cooperative Arapesh people and their opposites, the violent, competitive Mundugumors.

6. **(c)** The debate over abortion is nothing new. The ancient Assyrians outlawed abortion while allowing infanticide (which rid the world of unwanted female children). Greeks and Romans allowed abortion as long as it was approved by the husband, but Jewish law forbade it. Thomas Aquinas (1225–1274) decreed that the soul of a fetus was not fully formed until 40 days after conception. This allowed for miscarriage without damnation of the fetus, and it meant that for a long time, contraception was a worse sin than abortion. In 1869, Pope Pius IX revived the old debate and declared that the soul enters the body at the moment of conception. Thus, not only is abortion murder, according to the Church, but the soul of the fetus, unbaptized in Christ, is necessarily condemned to hell for all eternity.

7. **(c)** Saint Augustine wrote of the need for celibacy in those who would follow Christ. His words engagingly show the tension between the life of the mind and the life of the flesh: "Give me chastity—but not yet." A serious movement to make celibacy a standard for priests and monks began in the East with Cyril and Methodius, Greek missionaries in the ninth century. Throughout the debate over celibacy, the issue revolved around the fall from Eden — it was assumed that Adam and Eve had no lust until the fall, and a return to the innocence of the Garden was the goal. Leo IX (Pope 1048–1054) recommended chastity for priests, but Gregory VII *ordered* it. Resistance was widespread, and clashes between monks and married priests were often violent. Eventually many of Gregory's reforms were defeated and an antipope (Clement III) was established, but the clergy was directed to refrain from marriage

from that time on. Among the reforms of Martin Luther (1483–1546) in his split from the Church was the removal of this "dangerous and unnatural" prohibition.

8. **(b)** Strict followers of the Koran will find in it an proscription against intercourse during pregnancy. Since for centuries Catholicism considered procreation the only acceptable reason for intercourse, there was clearly no point to sex during pregnancy, and many Catholics were therefore encouraged to abstain from sex at that time. Victorians often avoided sex during pregnancy for fear of marking the fetus in some way, and even in this century, some doctors have advised against it for fear of miscarriage or fetal damage.

9. **(a)** Polygamy is marriage to more than one spouse. Its most common form, polygyny, is marriage to more than one woman. Polygyny was practiced by cultures as varied as the Chinese, the Babylonians, and the Mormons, as well as by the Hebrews of Biblical times. David married Abigail and Ahinoam after his first wife, Michal, was given by her father to another man. Polyandry, marriage to more than one man, is much rarer, and usually took place only in cultures where poverty or plague made it necessary. In the *Mahabharata*, an Indian epic, the princess Draupadi is brought home by the hero to marry him and his four brothers.

10. **(c)** The Talmud, the compilation of Jewish law, condemns to death those who participate in homosexual acts. The Biblical city of Sodom is equated with evil in part because of its allegedly homosexual population. (*Sex in History* goes into detail on how this association of Sodom with homosexuality may be based on misinterpretation. When Lot's neighbors tell him to bring out his angel visitors "that we may know them," they may simply mean *know* as in "meet" rather than *know* "in the Biblical sense," as in "fornicate with." On the other hand, the fact that Lot offers to send out his virgin daughters instead seems to support the more bawdy

interpretation.) Christian persecution of homosexuals (almost always men) outdid previous cultures' censure. The penance given to those who confessed homosexual acts was severe. Thomas Aquinas was one of the gay world's worst enemies in the Church, with his assertions that the sex act was meant for procreation and anything else was unnatural, but Martin Luther and John Calvin continued to denounce homosexuality even after their breaks from the Church, calling it a sin against nature. As recently as 1975, the *Vatican Declaration on Sexual Ethics* referred to homosexual acts as "disordered." Organizations for gay churchgoers now exist in almost every religious sect; the most famous is the Catholic group known as "Dignity."

11. **(d)** Throughout much of Africa and the Middle East, the ritual removal of the clitoris with or without the labia is an ancient rite that is still regularly practiced today. The idea is to deter promiscuity by eliminating the source of sexual pleasure, a concept eagerly picked up by Victorian Europeans, who sometimes punished promiscuous women this way. Besides being cruel, the operation is far more dangerous than male circumcision. Another African practice still in use in some places is infibulation, the lacing together of the labia to prevent penetration.

12. **(d)** In Genesis 17:12, God tells Abraham, "He that is eight days old among you shall be circumcised." He presents this law as a symbol of the covenant between God and Abraham's descendants. Circumcision, the removal of the foreskin of the penis, was traditionally part of the puberty rites of Egyptians, Mayans, Aztecs, Incas, Polynesians, and Australian aborigines, among others.

13. **(b)** Diane de Poitiers (1499–1566) was mistress of Francis I of France and then of his young son, Henri II. She was enormously influential in politics and the arts. In cultures where women were generally uneducated

and powerless, taking on the role of political mistress was one of the few ways in which women could move up in the world. Thaïs of Athens (fourth century A.D.) became mistress of Ptolemy I of Egypt after Alexander's death. Jeanne Antoinette Poisson, Marquise de Pompadour (1721–1764), was set up at Versailles in 1745 and became a patron of the arts as well as an archenemy of Cardinal Richelieu. Under her guidance, France became embroiled in the disastrous Seven Years' War. Czar Peter I brought home the Lithuanian peasant girl who would later become Catherine I (c. 1684–1727) against the advice of his councillors. One year after he finally married her, she succeeded him on the throne. Later in the eighteenth century, Catherine II (1729–1796) reversed the trend by establishing *her* lovers in positions of power, going so far as to make one beau king of Poland (Stanislaus I).

14. (c) We now know that bleeding from a punctured hymen does not always occur when a virgin is first penetrated, but for centuries blood was considered the true indicator that the bride was virginal, and husbands from peasants to kings proudly hung out bloodied bedclothes to impress wedding guests following the wedding night. In some Australian cultures, the hymen was ritually punctured before the wedding, and the bride might be executed if it were found to be already broken. Female virgins have always been granted sacred powers, whether as the Virgins of the Sun in Incan tradition, the Vestal Virgins of ancient Greece, or in Christian tradition, where, as Methodius wrote in the ninth century, "the soul of a pure virgin may become a bride of Christ."

15. (d) The role of menstruation in procreation was recognized only comparatively recently. As with most incomprehensible events, menstruation was the subject of myth and taboo. Orthodox Jewish and Islamic traditions consider menstruating women unclean; they may not be touched during or for the week after their periods, at which time they must take a ritual bath to cleanse themselves. Many African and South American cultures traditionally removed a young girl from society at the advent of her first period and forced her into isolation until it was completed. Few went as far as the Carrier Indians of the Northwest, described in *Sex in History*; they sent young girls into the wilderness for several *years* after their first menstruation, probably as a means of preventing early pregnancy. *Sex in History* also mentions a curious controversy that resembles one from the ancient Greeks, many of whom believed that the touch of a menstruating women could kill a plant—nineteenth-century doctors debated for months in the pages of the *British Medical Journal* over whether or not the touch of a menstruating woman could turn a ham rancid.

16. **(d)** The poet Sappho (b. 612 B.C.) lived on the island of Lesbos, where she was married and a mother. She led a group of women devoted to Aphrodite. Her island home gives us the word *lesbian*, referring back to Sappho's supposedly homosexual band of artist friends. In fact, much of Sappho's poetry was dedicated to a young man named Phaon, for whom Sappho may have killed herself in the throes of unrequited love. Despite her masculine pen name, George Eliot (Mary Ann Evans, 1819–1880) was devoted for 24 years to a married man, George Henry Lewes, and lived with him as if she were his wife. Novelist Virginia Woolf (1882–1941) was married to Leonard Woolf, although both of them indulged in affairs with women. The writer Gertrude Stein (1874–1946) lived with her companion, Alice B. Toklas, for over 40 years.

17. **(b)** Although today it usually means masturbation, *onanism* really alludes to the sad story of Onan in Genesis 38, who is told by his father, Judah, to "Go in to your brother's wife, and perform the duty of a brother-in-law to her, and raise up offspring for your brother," the wicked Er, whom God has slain. Onan refuses to produce children for his brother, and instead spills his

seed, probably in an act of *coitus interruptus*. For this, God kills him as well, and that detail has been used ever since to connect masturbation, the intentional spilling of seed, to evil. Whereas many Eastern cultures accepted masturbation and even designed special masturbation devices and aids, Orthodox Jewish and Christian cultures deemed it unclean and sinful and still consider it so today. European doctors in the eighteenth and nineteenth centuries attributed all manner of diseases to the weakness supposedly caused by onanism; and Victorian cures for masturbation included chilling the genitals, tying children's hands at bedtime, and enclosing the genitals nightly in tight, spiked cages.

18. (c) Cross-dressing was popular in ancient Greece, where young male prostitutes often dressed as girls to win attention. Agathon (c. 450 – c. 400 B.C.), a poet, was only one of many men in the arts who preferred to dress as a woman. For centuries in Western civilization, all roles in theatrical productions were played by men, and from the time of the Greeks to Shakespeare's time, certain men won acclaim for their portrayals of heroines in drama and in opera, where female roles were played often by *castrati*. Lord Cornbury (1661–1723) was known, according to *The Gay Book of Lists*, as "the governor in petticoats." He often dressed in full drag, including makeup and wigs. Stella Walsh, born Stanislawa Walaslewicz (1911–1981), lived and won five gold medals in track-and-field as a woman and even briefly married a man. Only after Walsh was shot and killed in a robbery attempt was it revealed that he was in fact male.

19. (a) The YMCA had sponsored traveling lecturers on what was then termed "social hygiene" before the National Education Association called for a policy of social hygiene education in the schools in 1892. Not until 1914 did the NEA become involved in actually training teachers in what the International Congress of Hygiene had retitled "sex education." Sex education at the time usually involved discussion of body parts and enough about hygiene to try to prevent the spread of disease. In 1964 Lester Kirkendall and Mary Calderone founded the Sex Information and Education Council of the United States (SIECUS), which is a clearinghouse and policy-maker for issues in sex education. Even today there is no national sex education policy; only three states and the District of Columbia mandate some sort of sex education in their schools. About one-third of United States high schools offer some sort of sex education in health or science classes; local districts usually determine whether or not a program will be implemented, what it will involve, and at what grade it will begin. Although a majority of parents polled favor sex education in the schools, a very vocal opposition movement has kept complete sex education from being universally required, despite alarming statistics on teenage pregnancy and sexually transmitted diseases.

20. **(a)** *Eunuch* means "he who is in charge of the bed," and the term was once used to refer to the castrated men who guarded the harem, although now it can mean any man who has been castrated. For hundreds of years, eunuchs were employed as harem guards and as all-around chamberlains in the Muslim Empire and throughout the Orient. From the Renaissance until the eighteenth century, boys with the best soprano voices were castrated so that their tone would remain pure. Someone who is castrated is sterile, of course, but may not be impotent. To guard against any problems in the harem, therefore, eunuchs in the Muslim seraglio usually lost both testicles and penis. Castration has also been used as a punishment for sexual offenses, from the castration of Pierre Abélard (1079–1142) for his secret marriage to Héloïse to the routine castration of blacks in colonial times for offenses against white women.

21. **(b)** The idea of courtly love began in the South of France, influenced by the more frankly sexual poetry of Islam and codified by troubadours who sang for wealthy noblewomen. At first, courtly lovers, described in works such as those by Chrétien de Troyes, could consummate their love, and the union was usually adulterous, with the woman being married. As the cult of the Virgin Mary grew stronger, the ideal woman became more virtuous, and the ideal love consisted of a balance of longing and virtue that only occasionally led to sin. Still later, in the fourteenth century, the male lover lost the perfection of character once needed to enter the sacred realm of love and became merely a pleasure-loving aristocrat. This love ideal had little relation to the realities of medieval life, in which women were valued mainly for their ability to bear children and had few rights and little power.

22. (c) The prophet Mohammed encouraged polygamy, at least in part to help replenish the number of his followers after losses in battle. Provided they could treat all wives equally, followers were allowed four spouses. Otherwise, they could take one wife and a number of concubines. The Muslims followed the Byzantine example of segregating their women; in the upper classes, women were kept virtual prisoners in the *harīm*, or sanctuary. The Ottomans took the idea of the harem to its limits, with the sultan keeping up to a thousand concubines, ruled over by the sultan's mother. The Ottoman sultans rarely married, and the son who inherited the kingdom was simply the son of the concubine in favor at the time of the sultan's death. Mohammed II's Law of Fratricide, issued in the fifteenth century, allowed the successor to the throne to kill his brothers, thus ensuring his succession.

23. (a) The *Kama-sutra*, reportedly written by Vatsayana between the third and fifth centuries, divides love into four types: love of aspects of sex, love of intercourse, love returned by the beloved, and unrequited love. It goes on to specify seven types of sexual union, with detailed descriptions, lists dozens of sexual positions, and gives recipes for aphrodisiacs. The book was valued by Hindus, whose religion specified four Aims in life, one of which, *Kama*, focused on the pursuit of love and pleasure.

24. **(d)** The *droit de seigneur*, a practice followed by many civilizations in different eras, was popular in Europe until the twelfth century. It allowed the king or lord the right to have sex with the new bride of his vassal or serf.

25. **(c)** The cult of Dionysus, originally a Greek god of fertility and wine, was imported to Rome in the third century B.C. Originally the cult was limited to women and its ceremonies were deeply religious, but the Romans focused more on the god Bacchus, god of wine, during the ritual celebrations. Men were allowed into the rituals, which were held several times each month and consisted of wild, drunken orgies, often featuring homosexual rape of young male initiates and occasionally leading to the murder of the unwilling. In 186 B.C., the Roman Senate forbade Bacchanalias without official license.

26. **(c)** In the 1670s, a Dutch doctor, Regnier de Graaf (1641–1673), was the first to see an ovum under a microscope and recognize that it played a role in conception. What that role was, he wasn't sure: he felt that the ovum contained a complete and miniature person who grew in the womb. Others of his time believed that this miniature human resided in the sperm. Before de Graaf, theories tended to stress the importance of the masculine input: Aristotle felt that semen blended with menstrual blood to produce a child, and later Western beliefs held that semen contained all the materials for human life. It wasn't until the nineteenth century that the study of genetics led to the discovery that both men and women contribute to the formation of life.

27. **(c)** In 1810, the Code Napoleon made homosexuality legal, ending the practice of burning gays and lesbians. History reveals dozens of other civilizations that toler-

ated or encouraged homosexuality, including the ancient Celts, Egyptians, Sumerians, Greeks, Rome until the sixth century, and medieval Japan. In the West, the rise of Christianity led to the outlawing of homosexuality in many areas. According to *The Gay Book of Lists*, there are 23 countries in which homosexuality is still against the law (see Test 7).

28. **(d)** Early Egyptian contraceptives used by women generally included substances that either blocked the cervical opening (crocodile dung) or slowed the movement of sperm (honey mixtures). Some women brewed their own potions to prevent conception. Aristotle recommended using olive oil, and early Romans used goat-bladder condoms. Other methods included *coitus interruptus*, post-intercourse douches, and sneezing and jumping to force semen out of the vagina. By the eighteenth century, condoms were popular in Europe; in the 1840s, animal skin condoms were replaced by rubber, and in the 1870s, a German doctor named Mensinga developed a rubber diaphragm.

29. **(b)** During the late eighteenth and early nineteenth centuries in England, the Puritan movement contributed to the upsurge in repressive morality that, by the time of Queen Victoria's ascension to the throne in 1837, was firmly entrenched. Victorians held two sets of beliefs—one public, which held that sex was a bestial act, proper only for procreation, and one private, which led to one estimate of 50,000 prostitutes in London by the mid–1800s and an incredible rise in cases of gonorrhea and syphilis. Victorians went to great lengths to avoid public mention of sex and things sexual: chicken breasts and thighs were renamed; piano legs were clothed; books by male writers were separated on the shelf from books by female writers (unless the authors were married); and major works of literature were expurgated of their indelicate words and actions—bowdlerized, an act named after Thomas Bowdler (1754–

1825), a member of the Society for the Suppression of Vice.

30. (c) The cult of Demeter, or the Eleusinian cult, was popular in Greece until the second century A.D. and centered on the myth of Persephone, a maiden who was taken by Hades into the underworld. Her mother, the goddess Demeter, condemned the world to sterility until her daughter was returned, but Persephone was only able to return for half of each year — the fertile spring and summertime. The Eleusinian Mystery cult, like other mystery cults, focused on death, rebirth, and transformation — of the child into the mature man or woman, of the earth into its fertile period, and of the sperm into the new human being. An initiate to the Mystery would submerge himself into water and emerge cleansed. He would be subjected alternately to darkness and light. He would take clay objects in the shape of sexual organs and mimic intercourse with them. Finally he might witness a "sacred marriage." These activities supposedly made him aware of the cycle of life and how it applied to his own soul. Other ancient religions had rituals dedicated to fertility goddesses, such as the Mesopotamian Ishtar, the Canaanite Astarte, and the Roman Cybele. Usually, these cults would begin by focusing on the fertility of fields, with sacrifices made to ensure that fertility. Later, however, they came to encompass human fertility as well.

31. (a) The Taoist beliefs were based on the concept of harmony with nature, achieved by a balance of yin and yang. In sexual matters, yin essence consisted of female genital lubrication; yang essence was semen. Taoists developed detailed sex manuals instructing readers how to achieve yin-yang harmony. These stressed prolonged intercourse, which allowed the man to absorb yin, since women had infinite yin while yang was finite. Women were to be aroused and brought to orgasm, but men were to attempt to retain their semen so as not to squander yang. One such guide advised that ejaculation occur once every three days in spring, once every two weeks in summer and autumn, and not at all in winter. The manuals described sexual positions with exotic names such as Firm Attachment, Exposed Gills, and Mandarin Ducks. The Taoist attitude toward sex waned with the upsurge of Confucianism in the last two centuries before Christ.

32. **(b)** Margaret Sanger (1883–1966) was a nurse who became an advocate of birth control in the early 1900s. Her experiences working with poverty-stricken families led her to realize the need for effective contraception, though her belief, quoted in Tannahill's *Sex in History*, that America needed "more children from the fit, less from the unfit" showed that her motives were not beyond reproach. Sanger organized the first national and international conferences on birth control, lobbied for contraception laws, and opened dozens of birth control clinics. Her activities landed her in jail more than once, but popular sympathies were with her, and today she is acknowledged as America's most influential proponent of contraception.

33. **(c)** Not since the days of ancient Greece had male prostitution enjoyed the popularity it did in France in the nineteenth century. The toleration of homosexuality encouraged by the Code Napoleon, added to the flourishing of prostitution in the Victorian era, led to the rise of the *demimonde*, the court hangers-on of the Second Empire. The word came from a play of the same name by Alexandre Dumas *fils*. In the *demimonde*, wealthy aristocrats and businessmen kept prostitutes, both male and female, busy. Many of these male prostitutes were transvestites, often wearing false breasts made of sheep's lungs, and the money the best-known of them made was equal to that made by the renowned female prostitutes of the time.

34. (d) The penis ring, designed to ensure erection, was mentioned in written works dating from the sixteenth century in China. The rings were often made of jade or ivory and could be engraved with delicate designs. At the same time, Western travelers discovered the "Burmese Bells," small balls inserted under the skin of the penis. These balls both enlarged the penis and discouraged homosexual intercourse. Later, women began to insert similar ben wa balls into their vaginas; the motion of two or three of them made for a highly erotic feeling. Use of penis rings and Burmese Bells continues today.

35. (b) The painting illustrates one of the sexual positions described in the Indian sex manual, the *Kama-sutra*. Many Eastern cultures, especially the Chinese and Indian, encouraged provocatively sexual art. These paintings and sculptures were not pornography in the modern sense of the word, however; they were accepted by most of the population and were not illegal. It wasn't until the repressive atmosphere of the seventeenth and eighteenth centuries that legislation against sexual art became widespread. For more information on pornography, see Test 7.

36. (c) Almost all human civilizations—and some ape groups — have a taboo against incest, suggesting that the need to preserve a wide gene pool is in part instinctive. Rulers of certain civilizations, such as the ancient Egyptians, broke the incest taboo in order to emphasize their godlike status. Early Christians were forbidden to marry within the seventh degree of family, and in modern times incest is almost universally illegal.

37. (b) Sappho (c. 612–580 B.C.), was a lyric poet whose home was the Greek island of Lesbos, also the homeland of Aristotle and Epicurus. Little is known of her life, but many of the fragments of her poetry that remain appear to be love lyrics addressed to female students.

She is reputed to have led a school for girls on an island known for tribadism, or female homosexuality. The island's reputation was strong enough for the practice to be renamed lesbianism. Sappho's poetry greatly influenced Ovid, who believed it was erotically homosexual, and such later poets as Swinburne. Her work was burned in A.D. 380 by St. Gregory of Nazianzus, and in 1073 much of what remained was burned by papal decree, leaving only the 700 lines that we have of her work today.

38. **(a)** With the rise of Victorian prudery and the simultaneous interest in sadomasochism in Victorian England came a fascination with sexual flagellation. Flagellation was common in ancient fertility rituals, and self-flagellation was a means to religious ecstacy for certain Catholic groups. In the thirteenth century, religious group flagellation was widespread, and the Black Plague of the fourteenth century resulted in processions of public flagellants. One group formed an organization called Brethren of the Cross, which held that 33 days of flagellation, equal to the years of Christ's life, would result in salvation; this group was condemned as heretical. Whipping as pure sexual stimulation only became popular in the nineteenth century, however. Flagellation manuals such as *Venus Schoolmistress, or Birchen Sports* sold widely, and mechanical devices that made genital stimulation easier during flagellation were devised.

39. **(c)** According to *The Gay Book of Lists*, Pope Julius III (ruled 1550–1555) kept both his bastard son and his adopted son as lovers, elevating them to cardinals. The poem "In Praise of Sodomy" by Della Casa was dedicated to him. The writer Somerset Maugham (1874–1965) was a well-known homosexual. When Alexander the Great's (356–323 B.C.) lover, Hephaestron, died, Alexander planned to carve Mount Athos into his likeness, but died before the project began. Christopher Marlowe

(1564–1593), the English playwright, wrote of his sexual tastes, "All they that love not tobacco and boys are fools."

40. **(d)** Venereal disease has probably been in existence as long as human beings have. Early Egyptian papyruses record descriptions of contagious pimples on the genitals. Many people believe that Christopher Columbus brought venereal disease to the New World, and the Spanish made it epidemic in Latin America. In civilizations where prostitution flourished, so did venereal disease. It wasn't until 1897 that the organism that caused gonorrhea was identified, and that which caused syphilis was found in 1905. At first syphilis was treated with arsenic; not until sulfa drugs and penicillin were developed were venereal diseases brought under control.

BIBLIOGRAPHY

This bibliography lists reference books that can help expand your general knowledge in each of the eight categories tested. It is not intended as a complete compendium of available books on the subject but instead offers a basic collection of introductory volumes that are available in most public libraries and bookstores.

Test 1: The Female Body

Barbach, Lonnie G. *For Yourself: The Fulfillment of Female Sexuality.* New York: New American Library, 1975. Discusses female anatomy and fulfilling sexuality.

Boston Women's Health Collective. *The New Our Bodies, Ourselves.* New York: Simon & Schuster, 1984. A revised edition of the classic informative guide to women's health concerns.

Brietkopf, Lyle J., and Bakoulis, Marion. *Coping with Endometriosis.* New York: Prentice Hall Press, 1988. Information on this painful and debilitating disease.

Hasselbring, Bobbie; Greenwood, Sadja; and Castleman, Michael. *The Medical Self Care Book of Women's Health.* Garden City, NY: Doubleday & Co., 1987. Information on health problems of women.

Morgan, Brian L.G., and Morgan, Roberta. *Hormones.* Los Angeles, CA: The Body Press, 1989. Tells how hormones affect behavior, metabolism, growth, and development.

Stewart, Felicia; Guest, Felicia; Stewart, Gary; and Hatcher, Robert. *Understanding Your Body.* New York: Bantam Books, 1987. Guide to the workings of the human body.

Trien, Susan Namholtz. *Change of Life.* New York: Fawcett Columbine, 1986. Discusses physical and mental changes of menopause.

Test 2: The Male Body

Gilbaugh, James H. *A Doctor's Guide to Men's Private Parts.* New York: Crown, 1989. A guide to the workings of the male reproductive tract.

Madaras, Lynda. *The What's Happening to My Body? Book for Boys.* New York: Newmarket Press, 1987. A informative book for young men about the changing adolescent body.

McCarthy, Barry. *Male Sexual Awareness.* New York: Carroll & Graf Publishers, 1988. Discusses how men can enjoy sex more and overcome their inhibitions.

Money, John, and Ehrhardt, Anke A. *Man and Woman, Boy and Girl.* Baltimore: Johns Hopkins University Press, 1972. The physical and mental changes from childhood to adulthood.

Stanway, Andrew A. *A Woman's Guide to Men and Sex.* New York: Carroll & Graf, 1988. Discusses myths and truths of male sexuality.

Taguchi, Yosh. *Private Parts.* New York: Doubleday, 1988. Men's reproductive tract and what can go wrong.

Zilbergeld, Bernie. *Male Sexuality.* New York: Bantam Books. 1978. A matter-of-fact approach to the myths and reality of male sexuality.

Test 3: Human Sexuality

Bell, Alan P., and Weinberg, Martin S. *Homosexualities: A Study of Diversities Among Men and Women.* New York: Simon & Schuster, 1979. A Kinsey Institute publication on sexual and social experiences of gay men and women.

Blumenfield, Warren J., and Raymond, Diane. *Looking at Gay and Lesbian Life.* Boston, MA: Beacon Press, 1988.

A discussion of the history, legal implications, and lifestyles of being gay.

Calderone, Mary S., and Johnson, Eric W. *The Family Book About Sexuality.* New York: Harper & Row, 1989. Covers human sexual response, reproduction, sexual problems, and sex education, with a family-centered point of view.

Carrera, Michael. *Sex: The Facts, the Acts, and Your Feelings.* New York: Crown Publishers, 1981. A useful guide to sexual desire and response.

Landau, Elaine. *Different Drummer: Homosexuality in America.* New York: Julian Messner, 1986. Includes interviews with young gays and lesbians.

Masters, William H., and Johnson, Virginia E. *Human Sexual Inadequacy.* New York: Bantam Books, 1970. The classic guide to sexual problems and their treatments.

———. *Human Sexual Response.* New York: Bantam Books, 1981. The classic study of human sexuality.

———. *On Sex and Human Loving.* Boston: Little, Brown & Co., 1988. An updated guide to human sexuality and sexual dysfunctions.

Reinisch, June. *The Kinsey Institute New Report on Sex.* New York: St. Martin's Press, 1990. An up-to-date informative guide on all aspects of sex, in a question-and-answer format.

Voss, Jacqueline, and Gale, Jay. *A Young Woman's Guide to Sex.* New York: Henry Holt & Co., 1986. A discussion of the pleasures and dangers of sex for young women.

Test 4: Pregnancy and Childbirth

Bean, Constance. *Methods of Childbirth.* New York: William Morrow, 1990. Discusses various methods of childbirth from Lamaze through water births.

Cherry, Sheldon. *Understanding Pregnancy and Childbirth.* New York: Bantam Books, 1983. A guide for expectant mothers for the nine months of pregnancy.

The Columbia University College of Physicians and Surgeons Complete Guide to Pregnancy. New York: Crown

Publishers, 1988. Chapters are articles by specialists on all aspects of pregnancy and childbirth.

Eisenberg, Arlene; Murkoff, Heidi; and Hathaway, Sandee. *What to Expect When You're Expecting.* New York: Workman Press, 1984. A reassuring guide for expectant mothers and fathers.

Kallop, Fritzi Farber. *Fritzi Kallop's Birth Book.* New York: Vintage, 1988. Simple, understandable, step-by-step guide to the process of giving birth with emphasis on Lamaze.

Kitzinger, Sheila. *The Complete Book of Pregnancy and Childbirth.* New York: Knopf, 1989. An informative detailing of what happens during pregnancy and delivery.

McCartney, Marion, and Van der Meer, Antonia. *The Midwife's Pregnancy and Childbirth Book.* New York: Henry Holt, 1990. Discusses alternatives to hospital care as well as the basics of pregnancy and childbirth.

Test 5: Contraception

Chalker, Rebecca. *The Complete Cervical Cap Guide.* New York: Harper & Row, 1987. Complete information on the cervical cap.

Gordon, Linda. *Woman's Body, Woman's Right: A Social History of Birth Control in America.* New York: Penguin, 1977. Discusses the politics of reproduction from women's rights to family planning.

Guillebaud, John. *Contraception: Your Questions Answered.* London: Churchill Livingston, 1985. A British handbook in a technical, question-and-answer format.

Shapiro, Howard. *The New Birth Control Book.* New York: Prentice Hall Press, 1988. Discusses tried-and-true and newer methods of contraception.

Silber, Sherman. *How Not to Get Pregnant.* New York: Scribner's, 1987. An informative, question-and-answer guide to contraception.

Test 6: Sexually Transmitted Diseases

Clarke, Loren K. *The AIDS Reader.* Boston, MA: Branden

Publishing Co., 1988. Readings from science magazines on AIDS treatments, epidemiology, and so on.

DeCotiis, Sue. *A Woman's Guide to Sexual Health.* New York: Pocket Books, 1989. A question-and-answer guide to STDs and safer sex.

Edwards, Gabrielle. *Coping with Venereal Disease.* New York: Rosen Publishing Group, 1988. Simple descriptions of most common STDs.

Graubard, Stephen, ed. *Living with AIDS.* Boston, MA: MIT Press, 1990. Articles about the scientific and social aspects of AIDS by scientists and public health experts.

Kiester, Edwin Jr., ed. *The Better Homes and Gardens New Family Medical Guide.* New York: Better Homes and Gardens Books, 1982. An informative guide to health problems, including STDs.

Landau, Elaine. *Sexually Transmitted Diseases.* Hillside, NJ: Enslow Publishers, Inc., 1986. A guide to STDs for young adults.

Richardson, Diane. *Women and AIDS.* New York: Methuen, 1988. The impact and dangers of AIDS for women.

The Science of AIDS: Readings from Scientific American. New York: W.H. Freeman & Co., 1989. Articles on the origins, epidemiology, and social dimensions of AIDS.

Test 7: Licit and Illicit Sex

Austem, David. *The Crime Victim's Handbook.* New York: Penguin, 1987. Includes a chapter on sexual assault and rape crisis centers and information about spousal abuse and domestic violence.

Dalton, Harlon, and Burris, Scott, eds. *AIDS and the Law.* New Haven, CT: Yale University Press, 1987. Essays on responses to AIDS from the government, the private sector, and institutions.

Koff, Gail J. *Love and the Law.* New York: Simon & Schuster, 1989. A legal guide to relationships in the 1990s, with appropriate case studies.

Morris, James E. *Victim Aftershock.* New York: Franklin

Watts, 1983. Written by a judge, this includes a chapter on what to do if you are a victim of sexual abuse.

Mueller, Gerhard. *Sexual Conduct and the Law.* New York: Oceana Publications, 1980. Discussion of illegal sexual acts with tables of penalties.

Test 8: Sex in Cultural History

Ariès, Philippe, and Béjin, André. *Western Sexuality.* New York: Basil Blackwell, Inc., 1986. Essays on the history of sexuality by Michel Foucault, Philippe Ariès, and others.

D'Emilio, John, and Freedman, Estelle. *A History of Sexuality in America.* New York: Harper & Row, 1988. Discusses sex in the U.S. from 1600 to the present.

Klassen, Albert D. *Sex and Morality in the U.S.* Middletown, CT: Weslyan University Press, 1989. Discusses sexual attitudes in America from 1970 to today.

Lewinsohn, Richard. *A History of Sexual Customs.* New York: Harper & Brothers, 1958. A dated but still fascinating account of the history of sex in Western civilization.

Richards, Dell. *Lesbian Lists.* Boston, MA: Alyson Publications, 1990. Lists of information on lesbians in all walks of life and historical eras.

Rutledge, Leigh. *The Gay Book of Lists.* Boston, MA: Alyson Publications, 1987. Lists of information on gays, from famous gays in history to countries that outlaw homosexuality.

Tannahill, Reay. *Sex in History.* New York: Stein & Day, 1980. Sex in various times and cultures, from prehistory to the present.

Taylor, G. Rattray. *Sex in History.* New York: Vanguard Press, 1970. The impact of Christianity on sexual behavior.